Balanced
Assessment Systems

Balanced Assessment Systems

Leadership, Quality, and the Role of Classroom Assessment

Steve Chappuis

Carol Commodore

Rick Stiggins

CORWIN

A SAGE Publishing Company

FOR INFORMATION:

Corwin

A SAGE Company

2455 Teller Road

Thousand Oaks, California 91320

(800) 233-9936

www.corwin.com

SAGE Publications Ltd.

1 Oliver's Yard

55 City Road

London EC1Y 1SP

United Kingdom

SAGE Publications India Pvt. Ltd.

B 1/I 1 Mohan Cooperative Industrial Area

Mathura Road, New Delhi 110 044

India

SAGE Publications Asia-Pacific Pte. Ltd.

3 Church Street

#10-04 Samsung Hub

Singapore 049483

Program Director: Jessica Allan

Senior Associate Editor: Kimberly Greenberg

Editorial Assistant: Katie Crilley

Production Editor: Melanie Birdsall

Copy Editor: Deanna Noga

Typesetter: C&M Digitals (P) Ltd.

Proofreader: Wendy Jo Dymond

Indexer: Molly Hall

Cover Designer: Candice Harman

Marketing Manager: Lisa Lysne

Printed in the United States of America

Library of Congress Cataloging-in-Publication Data

Names: Chappuis, Stephen, author. | Commodore, Carol, author. | Stiggins, Richard J., author.

Title: Balanced assessment systems : leadership, quality, and the role of classroom assessment / Steve Chappuis, Carol Commodore, Rick Stiggins.

Description: Thousand Oaks, California : Corwin, 2017. | Includes bibliographical references and index.

Identifiers: LCCN 2016016026 | ISBN 9781506354200 (pbk. : alk. paper)

Subjects: LCSH: Educational evaluation—United States. | Educational leadership—United States. | Teachers—Rating of—United States. | United States. Every Student Succeeds Act.

Classification: LCC LB2822.75 .C456 2017 | DDC 379.1/58—dc23 LC record available at https://lccn.loc.gov/2016016026

This book is printed on acid-free paper.

SFI label applies to text stock

16 17 18 19 20 10 9 8 7 6 5 4 3 2 1

Contents

Visit the companion website at
http://www.resources.corwin.com/ChappuisBalancedAssessment
for downloadable resources.

Introduction

Things continue to change in the area of school assessment. In recent years, interest in and exploration of formative assessment practices has swept through many school systems, while controversy continues to mount and surround standardized testing programs. And most recently, with the passage of the federal Every Student Succeeds Act (ESSA), more autonomy is granted to states and local districts. We have created this leadership guide to take into consideration these changes and have put together a new resource that is based on an earlier publication, *Assessment Balance and Quality: An Action Guide for School Leaders, Third Edition*. We list here our major revisions:

- The overall presentation in this book is condensed compared to previous editions of *Assessment Balance and Quality*. The book continues to center on the core of the work to be done to build and maintain balanced local instructionally helpful assessment systems. Previous editions recommended seven actions local school districts take to put in place the conditions necessary to achieve balance and quality; that is now streamlined down to five organizational actions.
- Included with this organizational perspective are actions to be taken by individual school leaders to both support the five organizational actions and to help expand their personal leadership knowledge base and skill set in assessment.
- The intent of the book is to be used as a hands-on guide as much as a resource to be studied and read. We have pared down and simplified the activities intended as practice and aids to implementation.
- Both K–12 school leaders and faculties of leadership training in higher education continue to be the primary audiences for the book. Given the busy schedules of school leaders and candidates in educational administration the book moves readers into the core content more quickly, with less "stop and go."

About the Authors

 **Steve Chappuis** has served as a school teacher, principal, and district administrator in charge of curriculum, instruction, and assessment. In the private sector, he has helped small and large education service companies establish strategic plans for publishing and professional development. He has delivered presentations around the country to school leaders on the benefits of quality classroom assessment and how to implement local balanced assessment systems and has authored and coauthored books and articles on the same topics.

 **Carol Commodore** is an independent consultant whose special interests center on leadership, assessment, systems thinking, motivation, and learning. An educator for more than 30 years, she served as a classroom teacher, a department chair, an assistant superintendent, and an assessment coordinator. During her tenure as a district leader, she facilitated the establishment of new programs in the areas of balanced assessment and foreign language. Carol has coauthored three other books in the areas of assessment and leadership. Carol presents and consults for local, state, national, and international organizations across North America, Asia, and the Middle East.

 **Rick Stiggins** is the retired founder and president of the Assessment Training Institute in Portland, Oregon, a professional development firm helping educators face the challenges of day-to-day classroom assessment in the context of truly balanced assessment systems. Rick earned a doctoral degree in education measurement from Michigan State University. He began his assessment work on the faculty of Michigan State before becoming a member of the faculty of educational foundations at the University of Minnesota, Minneapolis. In addition, he has served as director of test development for the ACT, Iowa City, Iowa; as a visiting scholar at Stanford University; as a Libra Scholar, University of Southern Maine; as director of the Centers for Classroom Assessment and Performance Assessment at the Northwest Regional Educational Laboratory, Portland, Oregon; and as a member of the faculty of Lewis and Clark College, Portland. He has authored numerous articles, books, and training videos on sound classroom assessment, assessment *for* learning and balanced assessment systems.

Balanced Assessment Systems and Student Learning

What does it look like when assessment is done well in the classroom? The good news is that many teachers can already answer this question. They know that sound assessment practice asks them to do the following:

- Establish clear learning targets that form the basis for both instruction and assessment.
- Ensure that their assignments and assessments match the learning targets that have been or will be taught.
- Select the proper assessment methods to match types of learning targets.
- Create and/or select assessment items, tasks, and scoring guides that meet standards of quality.
- Use the results of the assessment in ways that are aligned with the purpose for the assessment. In other words, they balance formative and summative purposes to meet the information needs of all users of the results, including students.
- Provide students descriptive, useful feedback during the learning process, not just at the end of a unit in the form of a grade on a test.
- When appropriate, involve students in the assessment process as both an instructional strategy and a way to increase student motivation by developing students' ability to self-assess, set goals for further learning, and self-regulate.

Educators who do these things are *assessment literate*. Assessment literacy is, in part, having the knowledge and skills needed for effective use of assessment practices and results to both promote and measure learning. Our shortcut for that definition is "Doing It Right—Using It Well." Assessment literate teachers can fold assessment results back into instruction, integrate formative assessment strategies into daily instruction to improve learning, appropriately use different types of data for the decisions they make about teaching and students, and use sound grading practices to help communicate about student progress and learning.

The not-so-good news is that there are still far too many teachers who, through no fault of their own, assess the way they were assessed as students. Through a lack of exposure to sound assessment practice in both preservice and in-service, assessment practice in many classrooms remains what it always has been. It isn't that unsound practice is simply the opposite of what assessment literate teachers do; it goes beyond that. The reality is that when assessment is done poorly, students are harmed. Yes, inaccurate results from a poorly constructed test will lead to a faulty score and eventually to a report card grade that may also be inaccurate. A confused or unclear understanding on the student's part of the intended learning and acceptable performance can cause a mismatch between what the student delivered and what the teacher expected. But worse damage can be done: Student confidence and motivation can be harmed, possibly ending the desire to learn or even try. A faulty grade can be repaired, or a student might get a second chance on a test. But for students who have chosen to stop learning, those things no longer matter.

And when we as school leaders are not assessment literate, we also pay the price. Most of us have dealt with something like what follows, maybe more than once: a crying student in the office upset about an "unfair" test, the confused and angry parent believing his or her child has the short end of the stick when it comes to a certain grade, or the perceived need to defend a teacher in a public setting even if some of the assessment or grading actions appear questionable. Most school administrators have spent way too much time in these situations, sorting through the weeds of detail trying to find what, if anything, was wrong with the test items or precisely how an assigned grade was reached. Or, assuming a district policy on assessment and/or grading exists, if there was any violation from expected practice. It's rarely easy or straightforward. But it need not be that way.

Assessing learning is one of the most important jobs of any teacher. We've already stated that we know exactly what to do to ensure that assessment is done right and the results are used well. But if that is so, why isn't that common practice in all schools and all classrooms?

TODAY'S ASSESSMENT ENVIRONMENT

Assessment in schools continues to be a bumpy ride. The politics of testing seem to overwhelm its potentially positive role in teaching and learning. Debate continues about the federal government's role in education and the punitive measures of accountability testing. Concerns about the costs and impact of over-testing, the instructional time lost, the uneven playing field, what the written (and tested) curriculum should consist of, where it should come from, who should define *poor performance*, whether parents should opt their children out of testing programs, the cultural responsiveness of assessment practices, and the role of assessment in our schools in general are all real issues, and they play in most of our communities almost daily.

Furthermore, to achieve what began as a need for adequate yearly progress and what is now in many states pass/fail accountability grades for schools with attached rewards and punishments, districts and states have added more and more layers of both mandatory and voluntary testing. The desire to generate the data that is believed to be needed to improve schools has become a double-edged sword: What if we have more data but don't really know how to use it? What happens if we provide teachers item banks, but they either don't know how to use them effectively or the banks themselves are poorly aligned to what is taught in the classroom? Could the increased testing also increase pressure on teachers and schools to chase improved test scores at the expense of well-balanced learning? Or what if the increased amount of data we might now have isn't reliable, but we continue to make decisions about programs and students as if it is? And what happens if all our energies and resources are spent in pursuit of data at levels above the classroom, ignoring the clear research about the positive effects of day-to-day formative assessment at the classroom level?

Recognition of these problems is growing: The new federal Every Student Succeeds Act (ESSA) wants states and districts to examine their testing programs and instruments to decrease the amount of testing overall. But it's a bigger issue than that: Unless we are able to align a new, different framework for assessment's role in schools with the overall expectations of what schools are now asked to accomplish and produce, this testing turmoil is likely to continue.

ASSESSMENT AND THE NEW SCHOOL MISSION

The mission of the schools most today's adults grew up in was to begin the process of sorting students into the various segments of our social and economic system. Assessment's role in those days was to provide the evidence upon which to rank those who remained in school at the end of high school based on academic achievement. However, we have come to realize that many students who drop out or finish low in the rank order fail to develop the academic and lifelong learning skills needed to succeed in an ever-evolving world of work. And so schools were required to become accountable to leave no child behind; schools and all students were expected to meet high standards, narrow achievement gaps, reduce dropout rates, and make all students ready for college or workplace training. Schools have recently been released from the requirement that ALL students reach proficiency in math and reading, and although the Common Core State Standards (CCSS) cannot be mandated by the U.S. Department of Education, the commitment to rigorous standards and success for all students remains.

But as the mission of schools has changed, then so, too, must the role of assessment change (Stiggins, 2014). Instead of just providing evidence for grading and ranking students, assessment must go beyond tests and tools to include processes and strategies that encourage and support greater student achievement, especially for struggling learners. This can be done while also accurately measuring and certifying student achievement. To do this we need to understand how to effectively use and balance both formative and summative uses of assessment. Doing so will help link assessment in the minds of educators and the public to something beyond test scores and reports. The concepts we introduce and describe in the following are not time-bound; they can cut across shifts in legislation, educational policy, and implementation strategies. To us they are commonsense ideas that can weather the storms of a changing mission and in fact can help it succeed.

BUILDING LOCAL ASSESSMENT SYSTEMS FOR BALANCE AND QUALITY

A *balanced assessment system* serves a variety of purposes, uses a variety of measures, and meets the information and decision-making needs of all assessment users at the classroom, building, and district levels. *High-quality, accurate assessments* provide these users with the dependable evidence of achievement they need to do their jobs and improve learning. And recent research has shown us learning can improve when *students* are involved in the process and included atop the list of key assessment users—in a new school mission, assessment should no longer be regarded merely as something students passively receive.

Assessment balance can best be achieved at the local school district level, because only local educational agencies have schools, classrooms, students, and teachers. For example, formative assessment is most effective in improving student learning when it is a process conducted by classroom teachers designed to help students learn more—it is not a function that can be served well by the U.S. Department of Education or state departments of education. Local school districts are best positioned to coordinate all the various levels of testing, including classroom assessment, and in doing so balance their assessment systems to serve both formative and summative purposes. Local district or school leadership teams can achieve this balance in assessment. Current schools or districts can conduct an assessment audit that acts as an inventory of the assessment "big picture" (see Activity 2.1 in Part 2), teachers can learn the principles of sound assessment, and by exercising leadership in assessment, school leaders can begin to take control of an entity in schooling that at times seems beyond our control.

Assessment quality and accuracy are required if we expect the decisions we make based on assessment results to be sound decisions. Going to the trouble to develop and administer more tests without first ensuring that the results will be accurate leads to a "garbage in, garbage out" end product. To ensure dependable results, assessments need to be developed that follow five criteria for assessment quality. Figure 1.1 highlights the component of quality assessments; three components focus on accuracy and two on effective use. In Part 2, we go into this model in more detail.

With *student involvement* in the assessment process (Key 5 in Figure 1.1) comes proven yet untapped potential for increased student learning. It is with formative assessment strategies in the classroom, what we call "assessment *for* learning," where students are users, decision makers, and players in the entire process, where assessment becomes more about teaching and less about testing. If assessments are to support improvements in student learning, their results must inform students

Figure 1.1   Keys to Quality Classroom Assessment

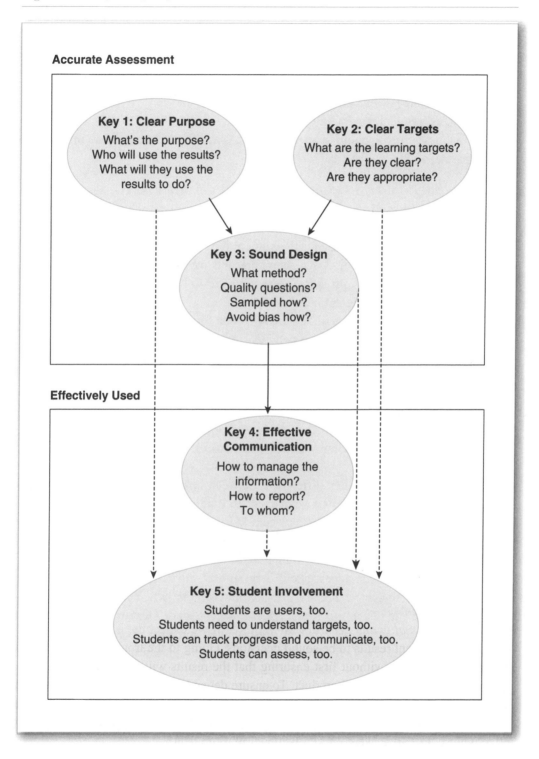

how to do better the next time. To do this requires communicating results in ways that are understandable to the learner and helps guide the learner's actions. Single scores and grades at the end of a unit or term do not accomplish this. We address this topic in Part 2 and provide a framework for student involvement in formative assessment.

INSIDE THE SYSTEM

To start with, a balanced local assessment system approaches each assessment given with these questions:

- Who are all our assessment users?
- What are the reasons they assess (purpose)?
- What assessment results do they need?
- What assessment conditions need to be in place for them to get the information they need?

Who are they? In classrooms they are teachers and their students, along with parents sometimes. Beyond them there are curriculum directors, school principals, and teacher teams who rely on periodic (common/interim/benchmark) assessments to provide evidence of changes in student achievement for program planning and refinement purposes. And finally, school board members and other policy makers and school leaders who do, in fact, rely on annual test scores to inform broad program, resource allocation, and sometimes personnel decisions.

What is the purpose of the assessment, and what form of assessment results do they need? As mentioned earlier, there are two basic options:

- Assess to help students learn more; such *formative* practice happens during the learning and delivers information to learners to help them see how to do better the next time.
- Or the assessor can gather data from assessments to certify that students have met certain learning requirements, termed *summative* assessment.

Figure 1.2 compares the key differences between formative and summative assessment. Teachers can use formative assessment to diagnose student/group needs, track student progress, and plan changes and next steps in instruction. And in a form that intentionally involves students in the entire process, teachers can use formative assessment to help students better understand their learning destination (where they're headed), their current achievement status in relation to the target (where they are now), and how they (the student) can close the gap between the two. This is called "assessment *for* learning." In this model formative assessment is not a test or an instrument but an ongoing interactive process in which students become partners with their teachers. Teachers provide descriptive feedback to students during the learning on how they can continue to grow, conduct assessment activities that directly involve students, engage them in setting goals for what comes next in their learning, and teach them to track their progress toward that goal.

And as the local system must have balance, so should the classroom also be in balance. A heavy diet of formative practice or a steady stream of summative grading events defeats the purpose and misses the opportunity for students when both formative and summative assessments are used in tandem.

Just as formative assessment in the classroom is sometimes mistakenly seen as just another test, assessment literacy is sometimes confused with being solely about data literacy. All levels of assessment produce data, especially if the assessment is for summative purposes. But crunching the numbers so that we can be data-driven is only part

Figure 1.2   Comparing Formative Assessment and Summative Assessment: Overview of Key Differences

	Formative Assessment	Summative Assessment
Purpose(s) for Assessment	Provide students feedback regarding; their own progress; support student growth through self-assessment and goal setting; plan further/differentiate instruction/reteach; identify students with difficulty or misconceptions; identify targets/standards most difficult	Document individual or group achievement or mastery of standards; measure achievement status at a point in time for purposes of reporting; accountability via grading or scores; graduation and retention decisions
Audience/Users of Results	Students about themselves; teachers about students, standards, and instruction	Others (teachers, supervisors, etc.) about students
Content Focus for the Assessment	Learning targets that underpin the standards	Varies by level of assessment: the achievement standards for which schools, teachers, and students are held accountable; daily learning targets of instruction
Place in Time: When?	A process: practice, instructional activities and ungraded assessments during learning	Event after learning: tests, quizzes, reports, etc.
Typical Uses of Process or Results	Provide students feedback to improve; diagnose and respond to student/group needs; help parents support learning; students track their own progress vis-á-vis the target(s)	Certify mastery; sort/rank students for gatekeeper decisions, grading, graduation, or advancement
Teacher's Role	Inform students of targets in a manner they can understand; build quality assessments based on targets; adjust instruction based on results; involve students directly in assessment when appropriate	Develop the test to ensure accuracy and comparability of results; use results to help students meet standards; interpret results for parents; document for report card grading
Student's Role	Self-assess, set goals, track progress; act on descriptive feedback and classroom assessment results to be able to do better next time	Study to meet standards; take the test; strive for the highest possible score; avoid failure
Primary Motivator	Belief that success in learning is achievable	Threat of punishment, promise of rewards

Source: Chappuis, Jan; Chappuis, Steve, *Understanding School Assessment: A Parent and Community Guide to Helping Students Learn*, 1st Ed., © 2006, pp. 17–18. Reprinted by permission of Pearson Education, Inc., New York, New York.

of the whole. Assessment literate teachers understand that data comes from many sources and in different forms and know how to best use each in concert with the intended purpose of the assessment.

And finally, as noted, the primary goal of a balanced assessment system is to meet the information needs of all users in the system. To do so we believe the *conditions* below need to be satisfied across all assessments students take. These conditions reflect in different terms the five keys to quality shown in Figure 1.1.

- The *purpose for the assessment must always be clear* to all involved. We must know who will use the assessment results and how they will use them, whether to support student learning or to certify it.
- The *learning target(s) to be assessed must be clearly, completely, and appropriately defined*. When that is in place assessment items and tasks and scoring procedures can be developed or selected to reflect the intended learning.
- All *assessment instruments and procedures must meet accepted standards of quality* to provide the dependable results decision makers will use.
- Systems must be in place to *communicate assessment results effectively*. In this way we ensure timely communication in forms that ensure complete understanding by recipients.
- The *assessment/decision-making process acknowledges the direct link to student motivation*. Doing so assists both successful and struggling learners to remain confident that success is within reach, if they keep striving.

LEVELS OF ASSESSMENT USE

Assessment is, in large part, the process of gathering evidence of student learning to inform instructional decisions. Local district assessment systems promote student success when they help inform decisions that both support and verify learning, that is, when the system is designed to serve both *formative* and *summative* purposes across three main levels of assessment use.

The primary levels of assessment are (1) day-to-day *classroom* assessment, (2) *interim/benchmark* assessment, and (3) *annual* standardized testing. Figure 1.3 crosses these use levels with formative and summative uses to outline the integrated whole of a balanced system regarding the many purposes it must serve. These purposes derive from the answers for each level to the same questions listed earlier:

- Who are all our assessment users?
- For what reasons do they assess (purpose)?
- What assessment results do they need?
- What assessment conditions need to be in place for them to get the information they need?

What follows is a brief description of the three broad levels of assessment, preceded by the following qualifiers:

- Over the last decade or so assessments given at levels above the classroom have been known by different names: Short cycle, interim, and benchmark are but three examples.
- Sometimes these names or labels are interchangeable or synonymous; sometimes they are not. One district may use an interim assessment entirely for summative purposes, while another uses it primarily as a formative assessment. One may mirror items from the state accountability test, another uses items that are finer grained, closer to the level of classroom instruction. So it is difficult to capture every level, for every use, under one or two labels and have sufficient differentiation.

Figure 1.3   Framework for a Balanced Assessment System

Level/Type of Assessment	Formative Assessment *for* Learning	Formative Assessment	Summative Assessment *of* Learning
Classroom Assessment			
Frequency	Ongoing, day-to-day	Continuous; periodic, depending on level of assessment	Periodic monitors of student progress
Key Decision Maker(s)	Student/teacher team	Teacher	Teacher
Instructional Decisions to Be Made	Student: What comes next in my learning? Is the target clear enough for me? What gaps exist? Am I ready to move on?	Diagnose student strengths. What comes next in my students' learning? What misconceptions are present? What needs reteaching or differentiated?	What grade or standards mastered go on report card?
Information Needed to Inform Decisions	Student-friendly versions of standards deconstructed to learning targets of instruction Diagnostic evidence of student's current place in progressions and of problems students are having	Clear and communicated learning targets to students Evidence of standards mastered and not yet mastered, and types of problems students are having	Evidence of student mastery of each required standard
Common/Interim/Benchmark Tests			
Key Decision Maker(s)	Teachers; students can assist in interpreting results	Curriculum and Instructional leaders, teacher teams, PLCs	Curriculum and Instructional leaders
Instructional Decisions to Be Made	Which targets/standards do we (I) tend to struggle mastering and why? What will we do about it? Opportunities for goal setting and self-assessment if students have access to results	Which standards are our students struggling to master and why?	Which standards are broad samples of our students not mastering?
Information Needed to Inform Decisions	Evidence of standards I have yet to master: the learning is not over	Evidence from assessments across classrooms of standards not mastered	Evidence of standards mastered across broad samples using common assessments
Annual Tests			
Key Decision Maker(s)		*Only works if results reflect student mastery of each standard* Curriculum and instructional leaders	District leadership team, school board, and community

(Continued)

Figure 1.3   (Continued)

Level/Type of Assessment	Formative Assessment *for* Learning	Formative Assessment	Summative Assessment *of* Learning
Instructional Decisions to Be Made		What standards did our students not master? What groups of students struggled? What interventions can be planned? What programs need retooling?	Did enough of our students master required standards? Did the school(s) make sufficient progress?
Information Needed to Inform Decisions		Evidence of standards not mastered	Proportion of students and subgroups of student mastering

- In addition, many schools and districts now use what they call *common assessments*, which are very often associated with the professional learning community (PLC) model (DuFour, DuFour, Eaker, & Karhanek, 2004). We call this out as an assessment layer between the classroom and interim levels. We do so because so many schools use this form of assessment and because, at this level, where teams of teachers are often involved in assessment development, assessment literacy is needed by those constructing the assessment and is as important here as it is in the classroom.
- To complicate slightly further, sometimes districts will apply the term *common* in front of the term *benchmark*, yielding a common benchmark assessment. In the end, it's less the name that defines the assessment than its purpose(s) and use of the results.

All this leads to this: capturing all levels and uses precisely would be unmanageable. So your school/district may have other levels, or use other names, in addition to what we have chosen to use in this book as primary examples of the various levels of assessment.

Classroom Assessment

Two aspects of the *classroom* assessment level are worthy of note. The first is that, historically, it has been largely ignored as a school improvement tool. The second is that assessment knowledge and skill are frequently missing from equations that define teacher quality and effectiveness. For decades we have invested heavily in local, state, national, and international standardized testing, followed more recently by increased levels of standardized interim/benchmark testing. During this same period, we have invested relatively little to ensure the quality or effective use of the other 99% of the assessments that happen in students' lives—those conducted day to day with their teacher in their classroom. Yet classroom assessment, specifically formative assessment, has proven its worth in enhancing achievement (Black & Wiliam, 1998). For this reason, no assessment system can really be in balance unless the classroom level of assessment is fulfilling its role in supporting and verifying learning.

Second, while classroom-level instructional decisions differ between formative and summative use, the essential assessment conditions remain relatively constant.

Achievement standards must be spelled out from the beginning of instruction in the form of deconstructed, clear, and appropriate learning targets. The learning targets must be reflected in quality assessments that yield dependable information with sufficient precision to reflect how well each student mastered each of the learning targets that lead up to the standards. Teachers and students can then know which standards have yet to be mastered (formative purposes) or the extent to which each student succeeded in meeting requirements (summative purposes). Both are important, but they are different, and effective local assessment systems balance the two. See Figure 1.2 to again review the differences between formative and summative assessment.

Common Assessments

Many schools use the PLC, or professional learning community model. A PLC can take on many forms and purposes suited to local context and need: professional learning, school improvement, school governance, and so on. But to follow the DuFour model and take advantage of combined internal expertise, often teachers at the same grade level or who share the same teaching assignments (secondary department level, for example) collaborate to identify common learning targets over a given period, develop assessments linked to those targets, conduct the assessments across the designated student subgroup, and then process the results together and determine next steps. By doing so they learn, in part, how they can improve their instructional program, which students or groups of students are in need of specific assistance, which standards appear to be most difficult, and so on. The purpose is to improve student learning through team-based instructional improvement across both programs and individual classrooms, using assessments common across classrooms/grade levels to do so.

Interim/Benchmark Assessment

While common assessments are frequently seen generated by teachers at the school level, interim assessments are often associated with a district-level focus, can have either a formative and summative purpose. In the larger picture, results can be aggregated across schools, giving a wider view of district progress, and allowing decision making at both the school and district level.

These assessments are criterion referenced, meaning they test students in relation to a defined set of knowledge and skill and can be used periodically (or simply beginning and end of term) during the quarter or semester to keep track of student progress in mastering each standard. These assessments can serve multiple purposes across three main areas: instruction, evaluation and prediction (Ruiz-Primo, Furtak, Yin, Ayala, & Shavelson, 2010). The primary purpose often is to identify those standards students are struggling to meet and those students struggling the most. This allows teachers to use the results in two ways. First, it provides them the information needed to improve their own instruction aimed at those standards. The focus is on immediate improvement. Second, these results can help teachers and students focus on identifying student strengths and areas needing improvement so they can plan assistance and interventions that overcome problems students may be experiencing individually or collectively. Note that if these are to be used in formative ways (that is, to promote further learning), accountability or grading decisions should not come into play.

There are two caveats here to note:

1. While the next assessment level (annual assessment, discussed next) is usually developed, administered, and scored under the direction of a state department of education, the first three levels described previously are under the direction of local teachers, schools, and districts. From that perspective the quality of those assessments is directly related to the assessment literacy of those developing the assessments and using the results, something that, unlike the state test, local agencies have direct control over.

2. Both common assessments and interim/benchmark assessments can and often are used in formative ways, but unfortunately for many educators these tests have come to be synonymous with, and the extent of, formative assessment. Although assessments at these levels can be beneficial (they can be used, as an example, to predict student performance on the annual accountability assessment), they are not the formative applications described in the research (Black & Wiliam, 1998; Hattie & Timperley, 2007). That centers on the classroom, guided by the teacher, involving the students, and is diagnostic, day to day during the learning.

Annual Assessment

When it comes to *annual assessment*, tradition has centered on summative accountability decisions: Did enough students succeed at mastering state standards? Is each school performing and producing successful students as it should be? But going further, in the United States since 2006 and under No Child Left Behind, these tests have resulted in school "report cards," with the data disaggregated to show how all groups of students are progressing and if at an "adequate" rate. The results are not limited to a single score report: The data is shown by poverty, race, ethnicity, disability, and limited English proficiency, this to unmask any gaps that may exist between groups of students. Schools that fail to do well fall into some mode of school improvement or correctives, or possibly even restructuring.

But the 2015 PDK/Gallup poll found that public support falling for this level of testing, both regarding the amount of time taken and whether or not a single score aggregated from a year's instruction should be used to judge schools, teachers, and students. The poll shows further that as a policy toll to improve schools the public prefers improving teacher quality over the use of testing to drive improvement. Still, these tests are not likely to be abandoned soon, and proper use of the results is at the heart of what it means to be assessment literate. Guidance for effective use is available from PARCC (Partnership for Assessment of Readiness for College and Careers) and Smarter Balance for those states involved with the CCSS.

ACTIVITY 1.1

Formative or Summative?

PURPOSE

Balanced systems blend assessments across multiple levels for both summative and formative purposes, each separated from the other by how the results will be used. Although it is possible for an assessment to be used in both ways, most are best suited for one use or the other, and in fact are usually designed for that primary use. In this activity participants classify each assessment type listed as either formative or summative.

This activity is a precursor to Activity 2.1, "Conducting an Assessment Audit." That activity asks teams to build an inventory of assessments being conducted in their school or district and analyze it on a number of levels. Understanding and agreeing on what is and is not formative or summative as practiced in this activity will help you conduct your audit.

TIME

20–30 minutes

MATERIALS NEEDED

None

SUGGESTED ROOM SETUP

No special room arrangements needed

DIRECTIONS

1. Make sure every participant is viewing a copy of Figure 1.4. Give everyone a few minutes to read the column headings across the top of the table and the row headings in the left-hand column. Notice that the right-hand column of the table headed "Is the Use Formative or Summative?" is left blank.

2. After everyone has reviewed the table, discuss each row to determine whether its use is formative or summative. Attempt to reach consensus on each example. If there is disagreement, team members should explain their classification rationale by answering the question, "What is formative/summative about that use?" Remember that many assessments can pull double duty, but for this activity the focus is on the use as given. You may find that some uses you classify as formative may also extend into assessment *for* learning where students are also involved in improving learning.

3. When you have completed your discussions, refer to the authors' completed form (Figure 1.8) at the end of Part 1. Discuss any differences of opinion.

Figure 1.4   Formative or Summative?

Type of Assessment	What Is the Purpose?	Who Will Use the Information?	How Will It Be Used?	Is the Use Formative or Summative?
State Test	Measure level of achievement on state content standards	State	Determine AYP (adequate yearly progress)	
		District, Teacher Teams	Determine program effectiveness	

(Continued)

Figure 1.4   (Continued)

Type of Assessment	What Is the Purpose?	Who Will Use the Information?	How Will It Be Used?	Is the Use Formative or Summative?
State Test (cont.)	Identify percentage of students meeting performance standards on state content standards	State	Comparison of schools/districts	
		District, Teacher Teams	Develop programs/ interventions for groups or individuals	
District Benchmark, Interim, or Common Assessment	Measure level of achievement toward state content standards	District, Teacher Teams	Determine program effectiveness	
		District, Teacher Teams	Identify program needs	
	Identify students needing additional help	District, Teacher Teams, Teachers	Plan interventions for groups or individuals	
Classroom Assessment	Measure level of achievement on learning targets taught	Teachers	Determine report card grade based on how well the student performs	
	Diagnose student strengths and areas needing reteaching	Teacher Teams, Teachers	Revise teaching plans for next year/semester	
			Plan further instruction/ differentiate instruction for these students	
		Teachers, Students	Provide feedback to students	
	Understand strengths and areas needing work	Students	Self-assess, set goals for further study/work	

Source: Chappuis, Jan, *Seven Strategies of Assessment* for *Learning,* 1st Ed., © 2010, pp. 7, 22–24. Reprinted by permission of Pearson Education, Inc., New York, New York.

 Available for download at **http://www.resources.corwin.com/ChappuisBalancedAssessment**

THE BENEFITS OF BALANCE

School leaders affirm that in good schools and districts little is ever done in isolation. A balanced local school district assessment system represents a comprehensive and purposeful approach to assessment in schools today. It is simply an organizational approach to assessment, the same way a curriculum is an organizational construct for learning expectations. But it provides intention and direction in meeting the expanded mission of schools. In doing so, the system finally will

- use the assessment processes and results to cause student learning, not merely report it;
- rely on multiple measures of student learning to inform decisions;
- spell out achievement expectations with more clarity, leading to more focused instruction;
- ensure each assessment at every level is of high quality;
- create an assessment literate instructional staff;
- identify and manage testing redundancies, gaps, and overlaps; and
- quantify the amount of testing students in the district undergo.

In summary, a balanced assessment system relies on assessments from multiple levels that work together in classroom, common, interim/benchmark, and annual contexts to inform decisions that both support and measure student learning success. The questions for leaders and/or leadership teams to answer are, "Are we in balance?" and "Do we have in place an integrated system of assessments that can provide the information needed for all users of assessment results and to help students both succeed and to demonstrate their success?"

You can begin to answer these questions and others regarding the current state of balance in your school/district by completing the School/District Assessment System Self-Evaluation found at the end of Part 2 in Activity 2.5. This is a useful tool to help determine where you stand now relative to assessment balance, quality, and effective use. We recommend if possible using a collaborative team approach to completing this exercise and doing it after you have completed reading this book.

LEARNING TARGETS FOR READERS

By reading this book and using the resources, our hope is to help local school district leadership teams to evaluate the extent to which their system is in balance. Once done, they can then identify what steps need to be taken next. The learning targets for readers of this book are aimed at serving that same purpose. Having now read Part 1, we hope the following targets are more in context and are seen as reachable:

1. Understand the benefits—the power—of balanced local assessment systems designed to serve the full range of purpose for assessment by both supporting and certifying student learning.

2. Understand how to evaluate the level of balance in current district assessment systems and build a balanced system based on quality assessment.

3. Become assessment literate, meaning understand the basic principles of sound assessment and the gathering of dependable information.

4. Know how to provide support to teachers (coaching, professional development, resources, etc.) as they face the challenges of day-to-day classroom assessment.

5. Be able to assist policy makers in understanding principles of sound assessment practice so they can set policies that guide sound practice.

THINKING ABOUT ASSESSMENT: SUPPORT RESOURCES FOR PART 1

The following resources that relate directly to the content presented in Part 1 are intended to either deepen understanding or assist leaders in implementing a balanced assessment system.

ACTIVITY 1.2

Embracing the Vision of a Standards-Based School

PURPOSE

Embracing the vision of a standards-based school might be difficult for some, both staff members and others in the community. In most adults' student experience, moving to the next grade was based on seat time and doing passing work on tests and activities in the subject areas. In a standards-based school, student success is contingent on mastering a set of standards that progress through the grades until students reach mastery on the standards for graduation in various content areas. In this activity, leaders consider what it will take to help all members of the school system adopt a universal vision of standards-based schooling.

TIME

30 minutes

MATERIALS NEEDED

Materials to record the discussion

SUGGESTED ROOM SETUP

Tables and chairs for easy discussion among participants

DIRECTIONS

As leaders, determine what talking points to share with teachers, parents, and the community to help them understand what a standards-based school is and what it means for the students who attend it, for the adults who work in it, and for the parents and the community who support it. Considering the following questions will assist you:

- What is a standards-based school, and how is it the same and different from the schools of our past?
- If mastery of the standards that progress to graduation is necessary for our students, what implications does this have for the following:
  - The written curriculum that is developed
  - The use of the written curriculum in the classrooms
  - The assessments that are developed and used
  - The instruction used with students
  - Reporting and grading students' learning
  - Hiring new teachers
  - Evaluating teaching
  - Determining needed professional development
  - Determining when a student progresses to the next level of standards
  - The assistance provided to students who have difficulty progressing

- Noting the implications, what beliefs that people currently have about their schools will have to be addressed?
- Noting the implications, what professional development, new learning, or other processes will be necessary to embrace this new vision of a standards-based school?
  - By the students
  - By the teachers
  - By the parents
  - By the community
  - By you as leaders

 Available for download at **http://www.resources.corwin.com/ChappuisBalancedAssessment**

ACTIVITY 1.3

Discussing Key Assessment Concepts With Faculty

PURPOSE

This activity is designed for use by building-level leaders to engage staff in brief introductory discussions of three key concepts: student involvement, assessment accuracy, and the learning team professional development model.

TIME

20–30 minutes for each concept

MATERIALS NEEDED

A copy of the selected reading for each participant

SUGGESTED ROOM SETUP

Tables and chairs set for ease of discussion among participants

CONTEXT

This activity includes three readings: "Engaging Students in the Assessment Process," "Assessment Accuracy," and "Developing Assessment Literacy and Competency." These brief pieces have been adapted from a series of readings written by Charles Osborne, Director of Assessment, Burleson (TX) Intermediate School District, for principals in his district to use with staff to engage in conversations about classroom assessment. This district uses the text *Classroom Assessment* for *Student Learning* (J. Chappuis, Stiggins, Chappuis, & Arter, 2012) with learning teams as the primary professional development model for developing classroom assessment expertise. The readings and discussions are one part of the district's multiyear support for school principals as they build awareness of the need with their faculties. The first two readings introduce ideas taught in *Classroom Assessment* for *Student Learning*. The third selection introduces the learning team approach to developing classroom assessment expertise.

DIRECTIONS

1. Each reading is preceded by notes for the discussion leader and followed by one or more discussion questions, labeled "Personal Reflection." You can use one, two, or all three of the readings, depending on the topics you wish to introduce to your staff. You may want to use the discussion questions that follow each reading and may also want to create one or more that relate the content to your own context.

2. Identify which of the three readings you will use. Copy the text of the reading for participants.

3. Distribute the reading, either at the beginning of the meeting or in advance. (If participants are to read it during the meeting, allow an additional 10 minutes.)

4. Ask participants to discuss their thoughts about the content of the reading and their responses to the "Personal Reflection" questions (or your own discussion questions) in small groups and then open the discussion up to the large group.

Reading 1: Engaging Students in the Assessment Process

Notes for the Discussion Leader

This reading (Figure 1.5) briefly describes four sequential avenues for student involvement. As we succeed in getting students actively engaged in the classroom assessment process a different dynamic begins to work. We begin to see that not only a balance of assessment *of* and *for* learning but also the assessment activities, with student involvement, actually form a bond with the instructional process and we start to see assessment *as* learning. This is when the role of assessment goes beyond the measurement of learning to serve as an instrument of instruction and learning. This is most evident when students are directly involved in informal classroom assessment activities, which serve not only to inform teacher and students of the learning at a given point in time but also as tools to enhance student understanding and learning.

This is an aspect of assessment that we will scarcely see until students are actively involved in the classroom assessment process. When this happens, the connection between classroom instruction and classroom assessment takes on a new dimension. At times it will be difficult to draw a clear line defining if an activity is an instructional strategy or an assessment strategy. We will arrive here as we continue to advance in broadening and improving our classroom assessment and increasing students' involvement in the assessment process.

Figure 1.5   Engaging Students in the Assessment Process

The idea that we need to include and engage students in the assessment process can generate a number of questions and conflicting understandings. Is student involvement in place if you let the students grade their own papers? Does student involvement mean that students write the tests? These are two examples of the misunderstanding that surround this concept of student involvement.

If we are to succeed in transforming from a teaching organization to a learning organization, it becomes essential that learners become actively involved in the assessment process. How can we become a learning organization if learners are not involved in assessment of the learning? How can we ensure that the learner is involved in a way to enhance learning? In this reading we are going to look at the meaning of including and engaging students in the assessment process. We look at four avenues within the process where student involvement is most important.

Clearly Defined and Understood Learning Targets

The first avenue of student involvement coincides with one of classroom assessment's core competencies: the importance of clearly defined, articulated, and understood learning targets. While a clear learning target is vitally important to high-quality teaching, it is also essential to achieving high-quality learning. When students know and understand the intended learning, their ability to hit that target greatly increases. Developing and writing the targets is the first stage, but the ultimate benefactors of clear targets are the students. A simple method to gauge this is to ask students about the learning targets. Either of the questions "What are you learning?" or "Why are you doing this activity?" should generate a response that includes a description of the learning target.

Student Self-Assessment

The second avenue of student involvement lies in students possessing and practicing the skill of self-assessment relative to the demands of the learning target. This is a skill that must be taught. Self-assessment involves far more than "find the ones you got wrong and correct them." It involves students evaluating their work against the clear learning target by using their understanding of that target and the samples of quality and problematic work provided by the teacher. To maximize learning, this self-assessment occurs prior to turning in an assessment, with opportunities to revise their work before it is graded.

Tracking Their Own Progress

The third avenue of student involvement leads to students tracking their progress in learning through record keeping of that progress. In the acquisition of any knowledge or skill there is a learning progression through which learners pass. As they progress upward toward the knowledge and skill demanded by the state standards, the clear learning targets provide the ladder of ascension. Learners should be able to accurately track the progress of their learning, where they currently stand on the ladder, and the next steps in learning to ascend higher. This practice of tracking learning—whether through the use of a portfolio, tracking progress on individual learning targets, or some other method—serves as a powerful motivator to students to continue improving. It allows them to clearly recognize progress and instills a hope and anticipation of further learning and success. Students' anxiety over report cards or surprise at the results is a clear indication that they have not been tracking their learning through the assessment process.

(Continued)

Figure 1.5   (Continued)

Communicating About Their Learning to Others

The fourth avenue of student involvement involves students clearly and accurately communicating about their learning progress to others. When they understand the learning targets, competently assess their own strengths and areas for improvement, and track their progress toward standards, communication of that progress becomes a powerful tool. Student-led parent conferences serve as a validation of student effort, confirmation of student progress, affirmation of student competence, and motivation for further learning. These conferences can range from total failure and disaster to exhilarating success. Which it will be hinges on whether students engaged in the actions described by the first three avenues. Student-led parent conferences with students who are not actively involved in the assessment process are a waste of time for the teacher, a source of embarrassment for the learner, and a cause of confusion or frustration for the parent. Conversely, a student-led parent conference where the student has been actively involved is a formula for satisfaction for the teacher, pride for the learner, and joy for the parent.

Source: Adapted with permission from Charles Osborne, Burleson Independent School District, Burleson, TX.

Personal Reflection

1. Do we have a method in place to determine that students truly understand and can articulate the learning targets they are responsible for mastering?

2. Am I actively cultivating the skills of self-assessment in my students? Where will I start in teaching these skills?

3. Are students able to track their progress toward mastery of the learning targets? Do I have one or more processes in place to help them do that?

4. What opportunities do students currently have to share their progress with others? What might we do to enhance those experiences for teachers, students, and parents?

Reading 2: Assessment Accuracy

Notes for the Discussion Leader

When it comes to classroom assessment, quantity does not guarantee quality. Although more frequent assessment can improve student achievement, frequent administration of inaccurate assessments holds little hope of improving student achievement. It would be somewhat similar to trying to lose weight and stepping on an inaccurate scale every day. And relying on textbook or other purchased assessments is also no guarantee of quality. This reading (Figure 1.6) introduces the three keys to classroom assessment quality—clear purpose, clear targets, and sound design—that are crucial to accuracy of results. (The other two keys—effective communication and student involvement—make up the "Effective Use" portion of the keys to assessment quality.)

As we make progress in using classroom assessment *for* learning, we must not assume that we can rely on already-developed assessments to ensure accuracy. For classroom assessment to deliver on the promise of unparalleled improvement in student performance and motivation, each teacher and administrator must invest time to learn how to evaluate assessments for quality.

Personal Reflection Questions for the Discussion Leader: As an instructional leader can I also serve as the assessment leader? How can I invest in my teachers becoming assessment literate regarding the quality of the assessments used daily? Am I able to review assessments and evaluate their quality?

Figure 1.6   Assessment Accuracy

Although following the principles and practices of classroom assessment for learning is an essential component in the process of improving student performance, the quality of those classroom assessments is not a neutral factor in the equation. If we attempt to practice assessment *for* learning with poor-quality assessments, we weaken our potential impact. Quality trumps quantity in classroom assessments when improving student learning is the primary value.

Assessment Purpose

The first key to accuracy addresses the intended purpose of the assessment. It asks two questions: "Who is going to use this information?" and "How will they use it?" You may be the person using the information, and you may be gathering it to determine a grade, diagnose learning levels, monitor progress, audit the curriculum, group students by needs, sort students for intervention, or any of a plethora of other purposes. Additionally, you may want the information to function as feedback to students, guiding their next steps, or you may want students to use the information to self-assess and set goals for further learning. It is important to note that a single assessment may not be capable of serving a multitude of purposes, because the resulting data may be inadequate or even inaccurate for the decisions we attempt to make. If we are going to have a quality assessment, we must first have a clearly defined purpose of that assignment or assessment—we must determine the intended uses of the information and then design or select the instrument so that it is capable of informing those decisions.

Targets to Be Assessed

The second key to accuracy focuses on the learning targets to be assessed. Are they clear? If the learning targets are vague, the quality of the assessment will suffer. Do our assignments and assessments reflect the learning targets students have had opportunity to learn? If our targets are unclear, or if our assignments and assessments do not reflect them, we are unable to accurately measure levels of student achievement or to accomplish any of the purposes we may have intended.

Assessment Design

The third key to accuracy concerns assessment design. Will the assessment give me accurate information about achievement of the learning targets that I can use as I intended to? This key has four parts—four "gatekeepers" to quality. The first gatekeeper is selecting the appropriate assessment method: Do we know how to choose assessment methods to accurately reflect the learning target(s) to be assessed? As educators we often tend to default to our favorite or the most simple to grade assessment method. Or we may defer that decision to the textbook or test publishers, which can limit what kinds of learning we assess. The second gatekeeper is sampling: Do the learning targets represent what was taught? Or what will be taught? Does the relative importance of each learning target match its relative importance during instruction? Is the sample size large enough to inform the decisions intended to be made, or is it part of a larger plan to gather evidence over time? A common error here is to include a mass of targets in a single assessment, producing insufficient data on any one target, which renders the assessment useless for any kind of "data-driven" decision making with regard to content standards mastered or in need of further work. The third gatekeeper is item quality: Do the assessment items themselves, the exercises or tasks, the scoring procedures and scoring guides all adhere to standards of quality? Do we know what to do to fix them when the answer is no?

Figure 1.6   (Continued)

Avoiding Sources of Bias and Distortion

The fourth gatekeeper is avoiding potential sources of bias and distortion: Is there anything in the assessment itself or in the conditions under which it is administered that could lead to inaccurate estimates of student learning? Do we know how to control for these problems in any given assessment method or context? Whether we are selecting or creating an assessment for classroom use, accuracy of results is dependent on the classroom teacher being able to answer each of these gatekeeper questions.

The skill of creating and selecting quality assessments does not come with age or experience. It comes with intentionally working to becoming assessment literate and competent. As we refine our assessment literacy and competency, it is our students who benefit the most.

Source: Adapted with permission from Charles Osborne, Burleson Independent School District, Burleson, TX.

Personal Reflection

1. When I use assessments in my classroom, do I consider the accuracy of the instrument? What am I doing to improve its quality?

2. Am I equipped to accurately evaluate the assessments I give?

3. What might I need to learn more about?

Reading 3: Developing Assessment Literacy and Competency

Notes for the Discussion Leader

This reading (Figure 1.7) defines *assessment literacy* as the possession of knowledge about principles of high-quality classroom assessment and *assessment competence* as the ability to apply that knowledge in the classroom to maximize student motivation and achievement. It then explains the learning team approach to developing both assessment literacy and competence, with rationale for why it is effective.

Figure 1.7   Developing Assessment Literacy and Competency

Assessment literacy refers to the knowledge and conceptual understanding of the principles of quality classroom assessment. When we possess assessment literacy, we can engage in informed conversation regarding classroom assessment, we can recognize good- and poor-quality assessments and assessment practices, and we can develop quality plans for implementation. *Assessment competency* refers to the consistent practice of high-quality student involved classroom assessment principles in ways that improve student learning. When we possess assessment competency, we can consistently *apply* the knowledge and understanding of assessment literacy in a variety of classroom settings and thereby have an impact on both student learning and motivation.

For many of us, training in assessment literacy and competency was not part of preservice education. Consequently, we may possess assessment literacy developed on the job and yet be lacking in assessment competency. As professional educators, each of us bears the responsibility for deepening our own level of expertise. We work in a district that puts great emphasis on providing professional development, but the responsibility for taking advantage of opportunities to further our capabilities lies with each of us individually.

Hands down, without any reservation, the best method of developing both personal assessment literacy and competency is through active participation in an assessment learning team. This professional development format requires three commitments: (1) to read a portion of the text selected for study, (2) to try one or more ideas out in the classroom, and (3) to meet with colleagues to discuss what you read, what you tried, and what you noticed as a result.

Assessment learning teams focus on the teacher as learner. They meet about every 3 weeks to review practices in assessment, to discuss reading assignments completed since the last meeting, at times to view videos, to share experiences, and to make plans for the next stages of learning and practice. Learning teams experience the greatest success when all members value and commit both to doing the independent work between meetings and to actively engaging in the collaborative work during meetings. When both these commitments are in place, assessment learning teams provide the very elements often lacking in other professional development efforts:

- They are ongoing throughout the year rather than a onetime training.
- They are job embedded and apply to our specific classrooms, grade levels, and subject areas.
- The content and meeting schedule can flex to meet the needs of team members.
- They allow team members to learn from each other as well as from selected resources.

Source: Adapted with permission from Charles Osborne, Burleson Independent School District, Burleson, TX.

Personal Reflection

1. What professional development have I participated in that has truly had a positive impact on my classroom practice?

2. What will I do this year to enhance my personal professional development in assessment literacy and competency?

3. Do I or would I consider engaging in team learning to enhance my assessment literacy skills? How can this approach help me become more confident in applying those skills in my classroom?

 Available for download at **http://www.resources.corwin.com/ChappuisBalancedAssessment**

NOTE

Figure 1.4 is the figure used in Activity 1.1, "Formative or Summative?" In Figure 1.8 on the next page, we have provided our own responses in the far right-hand column.

Figure 1.8   Formative or Summative?

Type of Assessment	What Is the Purpose?	Who Will Use the Information?	How Will It Be Used?	Is the Use Formative or Summative?
State Test	Measure level of achievement on state content standards	State	Determine AYP (adequate yearly progress)	Summative
		District, Teacher Teams	Determine program effectiveness	Summative
	Identify percentage of students meeting performance standards on state content standards	State	Comparison of schools/districts	Summative
		District, Teacher Teams	Develop programs/ interventions for groups or individuals	Formative
District Benchmark, Interim, or Common Assessment	Measure level of achievement toward state content standards	District, Teacher Teams	Determine program effectiveness	Summative
		District, Teacher Teams	Identify program needs	Formative
	Identify students needing additional help	District, Teacher Teams, Teachers	Plan interventions for groups or individuals	Formative
Classroom Assessment	Measure level of achievement on learning targets taught	Teachers	Determine report card grade	Summative
	Diagnose student strengths and areas needing reteaching	Teacher Teams, Teachers	Revise teaching plans for next year/semester	Formative
			Plan further instruction/ differentiate instruction for these students	Formative: Assessment *for* Learning
		Teachers, Students	Provide feedback to students	Formative: Assessment *for* Learning
	Understand strengths and areas needing work	Students	Self-assess, set goals for further study/work	Formative: Assessment *for* Learning

Source: Chappuis, Jan, *Seven Strategies of Assessment for Learning,* 1st Ed., © 2010, pp. 7, 22–24. Reprinted by permission of Pearson Education, Inc., New York, New York.

Five Assessment Actions for Balance and Quality

We introduced in Part 1 the concept and benefits of balance in local assessment systems. The three main components of *balance, quality,* and *student involvement* form the core of our systems framework. Without them in place, we risk assessing inaccurately, misrepresenting student achievement, and missing student learning opportunities when the principles of assessment *for* learning are not applied in the classroom.

Leadership in assessment begins with a guiding vision that centers on assessment as part of effective instruction—a use of assessment that seeks to promote student learning as well as measure and report it. School leaders who understand the necessity of quality assessments effectively used at every level will be better able to guide assessment practices in schools and classrooms. To that end, we encourage school leaders to consider five organizational assessment actions.

There are three actions to ensure access to dependable evidence of achievement:

1. Balance the school/district assessment system to meet all user needs.

2. Continue to refine achievement standards to help establish clear and appropriate expectations at all levels of instruction.

3. Ensure assessment quality at all levels to support sound instructional decision making.

There are two actions to ensure the effective use of assessment results:

4. Build communication systems and practices to both support and report student learning.

5. Promote the use of formative assessment and assessment *for* learning practices to build student motivation through the success of learning.

In Part 2 we explore each of these five actions; at the end of this section we ask you to conduct an organizational self-analysis. This will help determine which actions may be completed already and which actions remain unfinished. This evaluation will also inform a plan of action, a template for which can also be found at the end of Part 3.

ACTION 1: BALANCE YOUR ASSESSMENT SYSTEM

As defined in Part 1, assessment is the process of gathering evidence to inform instructional decisions. Balanced assessment systems meet the information needs of all decision makers from the classroom to the boardroom. Different assessment users need access to different forms of assessment results at different times to do their jobs and inform their decisions. Balanced systems serve them all.

We know that some decisions are made once a year and require annual standardized test results. Mostly these serve summative and accountability purposes: Are students succeeding at meeting standards? Are schools on target for improvement? Other uses of the results can focus on instructional program improvement: Which standards in which subject areas are students struggling to master? What percentage of students? What instructional programs need retooling?

Other instructional decisions come up periodically and require information from more frequent assessments. Interim and common assessments can serve this need. But at this level of assessment they may not all serve the same purpose. Some may primarily serve formative purposes: Which standards are students struggling to master, and what can be done about it right now, prior to the annual test? Which students need the most assistance and of what kind? Others are intended to play an evaluative role: Do the results suggest that this program of instruction should be continued, improved, or changed in any way? Can the results be folded in a student's grade record for the term? Being clear about the purpose of these tests from the get-go is part of assessment literacy.

And finally, we have established that the majority of instructional decisions are made moment to moment and day to day in the classroom. These require high-quality continuous *classroom* assessment results to support learning: What misconceptions are prevalent? What comes next in this student's learning? What can the student do to hit the target? These are the formative uses. Others serve summative purposes: What report card grade should this student receive?

If we are to maximize the achievement of all learners and close gaps between those who meet and don't meet standards, then local school district assessment systems will need to meet the information needs of all users of assessment results; that is, they must be in balance. This leads directly to the self-study question for this action.

Is Your Assessment System in Balance?

Balance begins with a differentiated sense of assessment purpose. There is no single type of assessment that can meet all information needs at the same time. The political, economic, and professional stakes tied to annual tests make them appear to be the single most important type of assessment that is administered in schools. While they are certainly important, they serve the decision-making needs of a limited number of state, school, and community leaders. The information provided by these annual tests only arrives once a year, while classes are in session all year. Teachers and students make instructional decisions every few minutes, so scores arriving once a year will be of little value to them. But this doesn't mean they aren't helpful to other users. It does mean, however, that there may be limited value in trying to have the results serve double or triple duty as formative tools, especially when the primary purpose of this level of test remains one of accountability.

Teachers are best served in their daily decision making not by large-scale assessment but by classroom assessment used to either support learning or evaluate it. With accurate information from formative and summative assessment both students and teachers can make immediate decisions about what to do next to improve learning and teaching.

As noted earlier, we differentiate the larger sphere of formative assessment practices from assessment *for* learning practices that are based in the classroom and involve students directly. Formative applications can diagnose student needs, monitor progress toward individual standards by individual students, and suggest changes in a teacher's instructional approach. Teachers' information needs are met and often are informed by results from levels of formative assessment both in and outside the classroom. Assessment *for* learning includes those things that teachers *and* students do, in the classroom, to inform teaching and learning while there is still time to act on the results. It helps students see and understand learning targets, helps them understand and manage their own progress, and uses self-assessment and goal setting to keep students connected to the targets of instruction.

In summary, balanced assessment systems serve formative, assessment *for* learning, and summative purposes by blending quality assessment use at the classroom level with interim/benchmark assessment, common assessments if in use, and annual testing. Balanced systems also seek to avoid making high-stakes decisions about students on the basis of a single score from a single test. This action asks you to examine current levels of balance in your system and how to plan for movement toward greater balance if needed. See Figure 2.1 to help you think about the current state of balance in your school/district.

Strategies for Balancing Assessment Systems

The leaders of the Elmbrook School District in Brookfield, Wisconsin, were committed to creating a sound and balanced assessment system. The leaders knew that to develop

Figure 2.1   Framework for a Balanced Assessment System

Level/Type of Assessment	Formative Assessment *for* Learning	Formative Assessment	Summative Assessment *of* Learning
Classroom Assessment			
Frequency	Ongoing, day to day	Continuous; periodic, depending on level of assessment	Periodic monitors of student progress
Key Decision Maker(s)	Student/teacher team	Teacher	Teacher
Instructional Decisions to Be Made	Student: What comes next in my learning? Is the target clear enough for me? What gaps exist? Am I ready to move on?	Diagnose student strengths. What comes next in my students' learning? What misconceptions are present? What needs reteaching or differentiated?	What grade or standards mastered go on report card?
Information Needed to Inform Decisions	Student-friendly versions of standards deconstructed to learning targets of instruction Diagnostic evidence of student's current progress and of problems students are having	Clear and communicated learning targets to students Evidence of standards mastered and not yet mastered, and types of problems students are having	Evidence of student mastery of each required standard
Common/Interim/Benchmark Tests			
Key Decision Maker(s)	Teachers; students can assist in interpreting results	Curriculum and Instructional leaders, teacher teams, PLCs	Curriculum and Instructional leaders
Instructional Decisions to Be Made	Which targets/standards do we (I) tend to struggle mastering and why? What will we do about it? Opportunities for goal setting and self-assessment if students have access to results	Which standards are our students struggling to master and why? Which students are struggling? What do the results suggest about future performance?	Which standards are broad samples of our students not mastering?
Information Needed to Inform Decisions	Evidence of standards I have yet to master: the learning is not over	Evidence from assessments across classrooms of standards not mastered	Evidence of standards mastered across broad samples using common assessments

Level/Type of Assessment	Formative Assessment *for* Learning	Formative Assessment	Summative Assessment *of* Learning
Annual Tests			
Key Decision Maker(s)		*Only works if results reflect student mastery of each standard* Curriculum and instructional leaders	District leadership team, school board, and community
Instructional Decisions to Be Made		What standards did our students not master? What groups of students struggled? What interventions can be planned? What programs need retooling?	Did enough of our students master required standards? Did the school(s) make sufficient progress?
Information Needed to Inform Decisions		Evidence of standards not mastered	Proportion of students and subgroups of student mastering

such a system would take time and long-term commitment. To keep this vision at the forefront of decision making—when and how to do it—district leaders created a simple tabular representation (Figure 2.2). Various levels of stakeholders had input in shaping the vision.

Figure 2.2 presents what the three types of assessment measure and the Elmbrook School District's primary and secondary purposes for the assessments. The first column describes the assessments administered once a year, developed by national or state testing organizations. The second column represents the common assessments developed by teams of grade-level or content-area teachers in the school district. The third column represents the assessments developed or used by teachers in daily classroom instruction. With national and state testing, the primary purposes center on accountability and program planning. With both district interim/benchmark and classroom assessments the primary purposes center on informing students for decision making in learning and informing teachers for decision making in instruction. With classroom assessment the primary purposes center on improving learning for individual students. National and state secondary purposes center on improving curriculum, instructional delivery, and goal setting for individual students. Interim/benchmark assessment secondary purposes center on program accountability. Classroom assessment purposes are entirely primary. With both district interim/benchmark assessments and classroom assessments the primary purposes are formative intended to improve learning for each student in the classroom or school. At the national and state level the primary purposes are both summative and formative in nature focusing on the system and aggregated groups of students.

Figure 2.2   Elmbrook School District Document Showing Balance in Purpose

Norm-Referenced Assessment	Criterion-Referenced Assessment	Criterion-Referenced Assessment
National and State	District	Classroom
Standardized Administration	Standardized Administration	Nonstandardized Administration
ITBS (Grades 2, 6) CogATs (Grades 2, 3, 6, 8) WSAS (Grades 4, 8, 10) ACT High School SAT High School State Reading Test (Grade 3)	K–2 Literacy Benchmark Assessment 3–5 Benchmark Assessment 6–8 Benchmark Assessment 9–12 Benchmark Assessment	Ongoing Assessment • paper/pencil • personal communication • observation • performance
Assess		
Reading, Writing, Language, Math, Science, Social Studies, Study Skills	All Curricular Areas (in development)	All Curricular Areas
Primary Purposes for Data		
• Reporting, sharing progress with students, parents, and community • Program accountability and comparisons of performance • Improving curriculum and instructional delivery of programs • Reporting to federal and state agencies	• Reporting/sharing progress with students and parents • Improving curriculum and instructional delivery for individual students • Setting learning goals for/with individual students	• Reporting/sharing progress with students and parents • Improving curriculum and instructional delivery for individual students • Setting learning goals for/with individual students
Secondary Purposes for Data		
• Improving curriculum and instructional delivery for individual students • Setting goals for/with individual students	• Program accountability	

Source: Copyright 1994 by School District of Elmbrook, Brookfield, WI. Adapted with permission.

Finally, one of the key actions a school or district can take as a foundation for understanding the current system in place is to do an inventory or audit of all assessments being used. In fact, the ESSA Act for 2016–2017 not only encourages this type of activity but funds it as well. You can find additional resources in the form of processes and templates at the Council of Chief State School Officers (CCSSO) website and at Achieve.org. Whether you use our process and template or another is less important than getting a firm grip on the inventory of assessments in your school/district. And, a complete audit should consider and include not only all the standardized testing in place but also assessment that is (or is not) occurring in the classroom.

ACTIVITY 2.1

Conducting an Assessment Audit

PURPOSE

This activity helps schools and districts map the "big picture" regarding what assessments outside the classroom are currently at work in the school/district. The audit acts as an assessment inventory, assisting leaders by providing information on what learning expectations assessments measure, when assessments are given, how much time each one takes, and each assessment's purpose, audience, type of data/report, and so on. Administrators then use it to manage their local assessment system, analyze its contents, and find testing gaps and redundancies relative to academic standards

The information collected through the audit is also useful when merging a local with a state assessment system and ensuring that they work together and don't overlap. Assessment audit results also are valuable when communicating with parents about standardized test administration and results. Once each test's audit data (time, purpose, standards assessed, methods used, scoring procedures, etc.) are catalogued, schools can use the information to create a letter to parents to provide them pertinent assessment information.

The activity has three parts. Each part contains a blank table grid for you to fill out with your relevant information. Note that this activity involves gathering information from a variety of sources.

Important note: You can create other grids suitable to your local program or expand the cells in the grids provided for a deeper picture of the total testing program in your school or district. As an example, perhaps the most important part of the audit is verifying that each assessment is directly aligned with the standards students are expected to meet. Once that has been done, you can check which specific standards are being assessed (and which are not) and create maps to help track which standards, the assessment method used, when during the year, how deeply, and so on.

TIME

Variable; multiple sessions over the course of a day or longer

MATERIALS NEEDED

School calendars or other documents that detail or list assessments being administered to students

SUGGESTED ROOM SETUP

No special room arrangements needed

Part 1: A Model for Identifying Gaps in Your Assessment Plan

DIRECTIONS

1. Once you have gathered your assessment documentation, categorize the details according to the column headings in Figure 2.3.

2. Examine the data to determine if the assessments are meeting the needs of all users.

3. Determine if there are redundancies in measurement of the content standards.

4. Determine in the overall balance of standards/targets measured; times of year for the administration.

Part 2: Record of Required State, District, and School Assessments*

The prior organizer helped you focus on the overall picture of assessment within your system. This organizer assists you in focusing on the use of assessments across grade levels and content areas.

DIRECTIONS

1. Using the same assessment documents as for Part 1, categorize the assessments by both the grade level administered and the content area being measured. Also, determine what level of the system requires their administration. See Figure 2.4.

2. Determine if there is balance in what is being measured across grade levels and content areas. Are some grade levels or content areas over-assessed or under-assessed? Is there balance in meeting informational needs—who is requiring the information and when?

*Part 2 developed with Dr. Linda Elman, Central Kitsap School District, WA.

Part 3: Assessments in Math (or Other Content Area)*

This organizer allows you to narrow your analysis and determine balance across any single given content area. This example uses math, but any content area could be the focus.

DIRECTIONS

1. Categorize the data according to the column headings in Figure 2.5.

2. Analyze the data for balance in purpose, users, and grade levels tested.

3. Do the assessments acknowledge all the users of the assessment information?

4. Does the assessment information meet all users' needs?

5. Are some grade levels under-assessed? Over-assessed?

*Part 3 adapted from Office of Superintendent of Public Instruction (1996).

Figure 2.3   Gaps

Name/Form of Each Standardized Test or Other Assessment Administered (list by content area or test battery separately)	Grade Level(s) Tested	Time of Year Given	Total Testing Time	Specific State Standards Assessed by This Instrument	Assessment Method(s) Used	Connection to the District Curriculum	Intended Uses and Users of Test Results	Communication Plans

Figure 2.4   Assessment Balance Across Grade Levels and Content Areas

	Math	Language	Reading	Science	Social Studies	Other	Total State Required	Total School Required	Total
Grade 2									
Grade 3									
Grade 4									
Grade 5									

Figure 2.5   Assessment Balance in Purpose, Users, and Grade Levels Tested

Test Name	Test Uses: Purpose	Test Users	School Level	District Level	Classroom Level	Time Needed	K	1	2	3	4	5	6	7	8	9	10	11	12

ACTION 2: CONTINUE TO REFINE ACHIEVEMENT STANDARDS

This action is all about clear targets. Well-defined and appropriate achievement standards are fundamental to sound assessments at all levels because they define what is to be assessed. We cannot dependably assess or teach to targets that are not completely clear and appropriate. However, we are many years into the process of establishing our achievement expectations, and it appears the task has not yet ended.

For example, the Common Core State Standards represent a vision of the meaning of academic success in mathematics and language arts and are currently the focus for teaching and learning in multiple states. Prior to that, most states had developed their own standards, and many professional associations have developed achievement standards for their academic discipline. They include but are not limited to the International Reading Association, the National Council of Teachers of English, the National Council of Teachers of Mathematics, the National Academy of Sciences, the American Association for the Advancement of Science, the National Science Teachers Association, the National Council for the Social Studies, the Center for Civic Education, the Geography Education National Implementation Project, the International Society for Technology Education, the National Association for Sport and Physical Education, the American Alliance for Theatre and Education, the Arts Education Partnership, the National Arts and Education Network, the National Association for Music Education, and the American Council on the Teaching of Foreign Language.

Given that, it would seem that what we expect students to know and be able to do would no longer be a moving target. But there may still be work to do for many districts to finally arrive at clear targets. Many standards, regardless of the source, do not represent a sufficient level of detail to inform instruction right "off the shelf." If the adopted standards do not yet guide daily planning and instruction at the classroom level, more refinement will be needed. By combining local district content area expertise with such resources as those listed earlier, faculty can create a more complete and unified vision of the intended learning. If this level of clarity is not met, quality assessment is compromised simply because quality instruction is compromised.

If refinements are necessary the standards needing more work can be deconstructed into learning targets to guide instruction. This scaffolding allows teachers to use classroom assessments to measure the learning targets on the way to achieving the standard, not just achievement of the standards themselves. These everyday learning targets form the basis of a teacher's daily curriculum. And one established, those classroom-level learning targets can be transformed into student-friendly versions that teachers can share with their students (and parents) from the very beginning of the learning.

It is important for districts to present a uniform picture of what is expected of students. Therefore, responsibility for these steps in the refinement of achievement expectations lies with states and with local school district curriculum teams or school grade-level/department staff, not with individual teachers. Qualified local teams or subcommittees can refine standards into grade-level or subject-area indicators and prepare student- and even family-friendly versions of achievement expectations. Now we explore all the requirements a little further.

What Is the Current State of Your Achievement Standards?

Clear, relevant, rigorous achievement standards serve as a declaration of accountability in what students must know and be able to do. Local standards or standards adopted from an external source should be all the following:

Clear	Clearly stated and understandable by the teachers and students within the district as well as by members of the community the district serves
Aligned	Where relevant, aligned with state standards for accountability purposes
Essential	Reflect what is truly important to learn; what is the heart of the discipline; what will have leverage in mastering the next level of learning; what will prepare students not only to do well today and but also well into the future
Realistic	The time, the conditions, and the materials are available for the students to reach the targets
Measurable	What students have to know or do is measurable and can be assessed accurately; that is, the outcomes in the standard statement are expressed in measurable terms

Here is an example: A group of world language teachers identified their priority standards. At the end of 12th grade, students will be able to do the following:

- Interpret the spoken words of the target language.
- Communicate orally and fluently with others in the target language.
- Read for comprehension in the target language and for a variety of purposes.
- Write clearly and effectively for different purposes and different audiences.
- Compare and contrast the cultures of the target language with their own culture.

Focusing on essential standards will not result in a laundry list of expectations that students or teachers cannot manage but, rather, will identify a manageable number of standards that students can and must reach and teachers can teach to and assess. These standards represent the heart of the discipline.

The world language teachers in our example further defined their five priority standards. They indicated what the standards looked like at the end of each course and grade level, asking, for example, What does "Communicate orally with others" look like at the end of Level V, Level IV, Level III, Level II, Level I, and at the end of elementary school? They determined that at the end of Level V "Communicate orally with others" is the ability to debate and hold extended conversations on various topics with different audiences using a variety of vocabulary and levels of syntax, while at the end of Level I this standard is the ability to converse on familiar topics such as family and friends using simple sentences and phrases with basic vocabulary and in the present or future tense.

Figure 2.6 provides another example of what can be done to refine standards, this time using the product-skill-reasoning-knowledge model of classroom-level learning targets. As an example the priority standard or benchmark is deconstructed at the Grade 1 level and at Grade 7, showing how the deconstruction of the same priority

Figure 2.6   Refining Curriculum: Classifying and Deconstructing

Standard/Benchmark:			
Produce writing to communicate with different audiences for a variety of purposes.			
Type: ☑ **Product**	☐ **Skill**	☐ **Reasoning**	☐ **Knowledge**
What are the knowledge, reasoning, skill, or product targets underpinning the standard or benchmark?			
Learning Targets: Grade 1			
Product Targets	**Skill Targets**	**Reasoning Targets**	**Knowledge Targets**
• Write sentences with varied beginnings	• Hold a pencil correctly • Print letters correctly. • Space words • Use lines and margins correctly • Stretch out sounds in words to create a temporary spelling of a word	• Distinguish the uses or meanings of a variety of words (word choice)	• Know what a sentence is • Understand concept of word choice
Learning Targets: Grade 7			
Product Targets	**Skill Targets**	**Reasoning Targets**	**Knowledge Targets**
• Write a personal narrative on an event that made an impact on one's life	• Write well so others can read handwriting • Do word processing such as touch typing, spell checking, and using various formatting tools	• Determine audience and purpose for writing • Select ideas that are interesting to the author and audience • Organize words, sentences, and paragraphs to make the ideas clear and the transitions smooth. • Distinguish among and select words and figures of speech that convey the author's thoughts and emotions to the reader • Determine whether sentences flow and have variety • Determine whether the layout is appropriate and the spelling, punctuation, and grammar are accurate	• Describe the elements of a narrative piece of writing • Identify the rules of capitalization, spelling, and punctuation • Identify complete sentences • Identify important events and know what makes them important • Identify logical sequence of events • Identify beginning, middle, and end of a narrative • Know strategies for drafting, revising, and editing one's own work

standard will spiral from one grade level to the next. The goal is to define success at the various grade levels in meeting the standard.

Student- and Family-Friendly Learning Targets

The same team(s) developing or refining the academic standards and deconstructing the standards can also write those targets in student-friendly or parent-friendly language. (See Chapter 3 of *Classroom Assessment* for *Student Learning* [J.Chappuis,

Stiggins, Chappuis, & Arter, 2012] for in-depth discussion of writing student-friendly versions of learning targets.) This process will unify the language being used with students across all teachers and classrooms. Having a common curriculum language will benefit students, teachers, parents, and whoever else has a need to know and work with the targets. Putting *family-friendly* targets on your district's or school's website will also help parents know what their students must master in their learning. It will make the classroom transparent to the parents and to the community as well and publicly declare your accountability in student learning.

ACTIVITY 2.2

Deconstructing Standards Into Classroom-Level Achievement Targets: Practice for School Leaders

PURPOSE

The goal of state standards is to set priorities on what students need to know and be able to do. Sometimes standards are broken down into benchmarks or indicators to further define the standard. But have you ever looked at content standards, benchmarks, or indicators and still been confused about what they meant or found they weren't specific enough to guide daily instruction?

- What do I need to teach here? What has to come first in order for students to master this?
- How do I explain the target to students so they will understand?
- Will my colleagues interpret the target the same way I do?
- How do I best teach this so students can do well?

We've found that when content standards are not accompanied by what can serve as day-to-day classroom curriculum, it's helpful to "deconstruct," or break down, unclear standards to see what knowledge, reasoning proficiencies, skills, and/or products underpin student success. Classroom instruction and assessment are then built around these deconstructed learning targets.

Note: This activity is designed to provide an example of a process for deconstructing standards and classifying learning targets. It serves as only an introduction, an illustration of the value of the process. We recommend more in-depth practice than we can provide here.

TIME

1 hour

MATERIALS NEEDED

- Interactive whiteboards or flip charts, markers
- Copies of standards, benchmarks, or indicators, or whatever level of curriculum that seems vague or unclear to teachers

SUGGESTED ROOM SETUP

Tables and chairs set so teachers can discuss and record their work

THE PROCESS

1. Choose a standard, indicator, or benchmark that is unclear—where it isn't immediately clear what you might teach or where teachers might have different interpretations of what the indicator might mean. For example, "Knows the binomial theorem" might mean

   a. Knowledge interpretations: (1) Knows it by sight—can pick it out of a list. (2) Can reproduce it when asked.

   b. Reasoning interpretations: (1) Can use it to solve a problem when instructed to do so. (2) Can choose the problems best solved using the binomial theorem. (3) Can write a problem that would require the binomial theorem to solve.

   Each of these interpretations would have different implications for instruction. Which interpretation is correct?

2. For your chosen standard, identify whether it is, ultimately, a knowledge, reasoning, skills, or product learning target. Each of these is defined in the accompanying list (Figure 2.7), "Types of Achievement Targets."

Figure 2.7   Types of Achievement Targets

Use this list to help you understand and identify the different kinds of classroom learning to be developed and assessed as students work toward achieving state standards:

Master Factual and Procedural *Knowledge*

Some to be learned outright

Some to be retrieved using reference materials

Use Knowledge to *Reason and Solve Problems*

Analytical or comparative reasoning

Synthesizing

Classifying

Induction and deduction

Critical/evaluative thinking

Demonstrate Mastery of Specific *Skills*

Speaking a second language

Giving an oral presentation

Working effectively on a team

Science process skills

Create Quality *Products*

Writing samples

Term projects

Artistic products

Research reports

Shop projects

Science exhibits

Acquire Positive Affect/Dispositions

Desire to learn/read/think critically

Positive attitude toward school

Good citizenship

Respect toward self and others

Flexibility

Perseverance

3. To help determine the *ultimate* target type of a particular benchmark, look for key words. Key words are shown in Figure 2.8, "Types of Achievement Targets: Key Words." For example, identify the ultimate type of each of the following standards:

- Identify words that have similar meanings (synonyms).
- Use clear diction, pitch, tempo, and tone, and adjust volume and tempo to stress important ideas.
- Keep records of investigations and observations that are understandable weeks or months later.
- Identify that hypotheses are valuable even when they are not supported.
- Classify ideas from informational texts as main ideas or supporting details.
- Model a problem situation using physical materials.
- Write, simplify, and evaluate algebraic expressions (including formulas) to generalize situations and solve problems.
- Evaluate policies that have been proposed as ways of dealing with social changes resulting from new technologies.

(*Answers:* knowledge, skill, product, knowledge, reasoning, product, knowledge or reasoning, knowledge or reasoning)

Note: Key words won't always identify the ultimate target type of a standard, indicator, or benchmark. For example, what is the ultimate goal of "Knows the binomial theorem"? The word *knows* indicates that it's a knowledge target, but is it really ultimately a reasoning target? Since there may be ambiguity on ultimate type, the first job is to come to agreement on what the standard, benchmark, or indicator means.

Figure 2.8   Types of Achievement Targets: Key Words

Target Type	Explanation	Content Standards/ Benchmark Key Words	Examples
Knowledge/ Understanding	Some knowledge/ facts/concepts to be learned outright; some to be retrieved using reference materials	Explain, understand, describe, identify, recognize, tell, name, list, identify, give examples, define, label, match, choose, recall, recognize, select	Vocabulary Measurement concepts U.S. government structure
Reasoning	Thinking proficiencies; using one's knowledge to solve a problem, make a decision, plan, and so on	*Analyze:* components, parts, ingredients, logical sequence, steps, main idea, supporting details, determine, dissect, examine, order *Compare/contrast:* discriminate between/ among; alike and different, relate, distinguish between *Synthesize:* combine into, blend, formulate, organize, adapt, modify	Think critically Analyze authors' use of language Solve problems Compare forms of government Self-evaluation Analyze health information

(Continued)

Figure 2.8   (Continued)

Target Type	Explanation	Content Standards/ Benchmark Key Words	Examples
Reasoning (cont.)		*Classify:* categorize, sort, group *Infer/deduce:* interpret, implications, predict/draw conclusions *Evaluate:* justify, support opinion, think critically, debate, defend, dispute, evaluate, judge, prove	
Skills	Behavioral demonstrations; where the doing is what is important; using one's knowledge and reasoning to perform skillfully	Observe, focus attention, listen, perform, do, question, conduct, work, read, speak, assemble, operate, use, demonstrate, measure, investigate, model, collect, dramatize	Read fluently Oral presentations Play an instrument Use laboratory equipment Conduct investigations
Products	Where the characteristics of the final product are important; using one's knowledge, reasoning, and skills to produce a final product	Design, produce, create, develop, make, write, draw, represent, display, model, construct	Writing Artistic products Research reports Make a map Personal fitness plan Make a model that represents a scientific principle

Source: Chappuis, Jan; Stiggins, Rick J.; Chappuis, Steve; Arter, Judith A., *Classroom Assessment* for *Student Learning: Doing It Right—Using It Well*, 2nd Ed., © 2012, pp. 27, 64. Reprinted by permission of Pearson Education, Inc., New York, New York.

4. Next, consider the knowledge, reasoning, and/or skills prerequisite to and underpinning competence of your selected standard, benchmark, or indicator. Ask yourself the following four questions:

- What does a student need to know and understand to attain mastery on this benchmark?
- What patterns of reasoning, if any, are required to attain mastery on this benchmark?
- On what specific performance skills, if any, must students attain proficiency to attain mastery on this benchmark?
- What products, if any, would students be proficient in creating if they were masters of this benchmark?

These form a hierarchy. If the ultimate type of target is *product*, then it has all four types of underpinnings: knowledge, reasoning, skills, and products as was seen in Figure 2.6. However, if the standard is ultimately a skill, then there will be only knowledge, reasoning, and skill underpinnings. Likewise, if the standard is ultimately reasoning, there will be only knowledge and reasoning underpinnings. And, like the nursery rhyme, knowledge stands alone. For examples of how this works, see Figures 2.9 through 2.12 on pages 44–45.

For example, you might decide that "Knows the binomial theorem" is a reasoning target. Therefore, it has knowledge underpinnings—knows what the binomial theorem is and when to use it. It also has reasoning underpinnings that need to be practiced—use the binomial theorem to solve problems, identify problems best solved using it, and so on. All these things should be incorporated into instruction.

Key Points to Remember

1. Not all benchmarks embody all types of learning targets. There is a hierarchy. Knowledge targets embody no reasoning, skill, or product underpinnings. Reasoning targets require knowledge but no skills or products. Skills targets require underlying knowledge and reasoning, but not products. Product targets might be underpinned by all four types of learning targets.

2. You are looking at what the benchmark requires students to know and be able to do, not how you will assess it. Because the import of this statement might not be immediately obvious, consider "Compare and contrast democracies with other forms of government." This is a reasoning target. It requires

   - knowledge of what a democracy is and knowledge of other types of government—purposes and how power is acquired, used, and justified; and how government can affect people.
   - practice in comparing and contrasting—a reasoning target—using the knowledge of different forms of government.

   You might assess these knowledge and reasoning underpinnings through an oral presentation (a skill). If you unpack the assessment, you get the following underpinnings:

   - As earlier, the assessment requires knowledge of what a democracy is and knowledge of other types of government—purposes; how power is acquired, used, and justified; and how government can affect people.
   - The assessment also requires knowledge of oral presentations, for example, the need to use language that fits the audience, have eye contact, organize the presentation in a way that the audience will understand (and the various options for this), and so on.
   - As earlier, the assessment also requires practice in comparing and contrasting—a reasoning target—using the knowledge of different forms of government.
   - But other reasoning proficiencies are involved in the assessment that are not required by the original standard, for example, choosing one's particular presentation style, organization, and props from all those possible to serve the needs of the current presentation.
   - There are also skills involved in the assessment that are not required by the standard itself: actually giving the oral presentation—modulating voice tone and speed, actually looking at the audience, actually manipulating props, and so on.

   To summarize, an assessment developed to elicit the desired standards might require other knowledge, reasoning, skills, and/or products that are not actually part of the standard(s) being assessed. So when you unpack a standard, you might be tempted to list all these. But don't. All this extra information is not required for the benchmark, just for the assessment. Any knowledge, reasoning, skill, or product that is required for the assessment that is not required for the standard is a potential source of bias that can distort one's ability to determine student status on the learning target(s) under consideration. The effect of these extras needs to be minimized or you won't know how students perform on the actual benchmarks under consideration.

Examples

"Drive with skill." This is a skill-level target. Therefore, it has only knowledge, reasoning, and skill underpinnings.

Figure 2.9   Learning to Drive a Car

Knowledge/ Understanding	Know the law Understand informal rules of the road, e.g., courtesy Understand what different parts of the car do; read signs and understand what they mean Understand what "creating a danger" means Understand what "creating a hazard" means
Reasoning	Analyze road conditions, vehicle performance, and other driver's actions, compare/contrast this information with knowledge and past experience, synthesize information, and evaluate options to make decisions on what to do next Evaluate "am I safe" and synthesize information to take action if needed
Skills	Steering, shifting, parallel parking, looking, signaling, backing up, and so on; fluidity/automaticity in performing driving actions
Products	None (undamaged car . . . ?)

"Distinguish fact from judgment and opinion; recognize stereotypes; compare and contrast historical information." This is a reasoning level target. Therefore, it has only reasoning and knowledge underpinnings.

Figure 2.10   History Example

Knowledge/ Understanding	What facts are and how to identify them What opinions are and how to identify them What stereotypes are and how to identify them What it means to compare and contrast things The basis (bases) or criteria on which to compare and contrast (events, people, conditions, events, consequences)
Reasoning	Distinguish facts from opinions in the context of news reporting Recognize novel stereotypes; find the correct information on which to compare and contrast Compare and contrast the historical information specified on the bases specified
Skills	None required
Products	None required

Examples From State Standards

"Students will evaluate different interpretations of historical events." This is a reasoning level target; therefore it has only knowledge and reasoning underpinnings.

Figure 2.11   Sample State Standard 1

Knowledge/ Understanding	Students must know and understand key features of each historical event and must understand each of the alternative interpretations to be evaluated. The teacher must determine if students are to know those things outright or if they can use reference materials to retrieve the required knowledge.
Reasoning	Evaluative reasoning requires judgment about the quality of each interpretation. Thus students must demonstrate both an understanding of the criteria by which one judges the quality of an interpretation and the ability to apply these criteria.
Skills	None required
Products	None required

"Students will use styles appropriate for their audience and purpose, including proper use of voice, word choice, and sentence fluency." Writing is a product level target; therefore, it will have all four types of target underpinnings.

Figure 2.12   Sample State Standard 2

Knowledge/ Understanding	Writers must possess appropriate understanding of the concept of style as evidenced in voice, word choice, and sentence fluency. They need to know what voice, word choice, and sentence fluency are; why they are important; and the ways they can vary. They need to understand various audiences and purposes for text and how these might influence style. In addition, students must possess knowledge of the topic they are to write about.
Reasoning	Writers must be able to reason through voice, word choice, and sentence fluency choices for novel audiences and purposes. They also must figure out how to make appropriate voice, word choice, and sentence construction decisions while composing original text for various audiences and purposes.
Skills	Students will either write longhand or will compose text on a keyboard. Each requires its own kind of skill competence.
Products	The final evidence of competence will be written products that present evidence of the ability to write effectively for different audiences and purposes.

DIRECTIONS

Listed here are several more state benchmarks. Pick one where it is not immediately clear what you would teach or for which teachers might disagree. Determine the type of target each ultimately represents. Then analyze it for the knowledge/understanding, reasoning, skill, and/or product prerequisites (as appropriate; remember the hierarchy) needed to perform well on the benchmark. Ask yourself, "What would students need to know and understand to perform well? What reasoning, if any, does this standard require? What skills, if any, would the students need to practice? What products, if any, would students need practice producing?" Practice deconstructing as many as you need to understand the curriculum development task at hand.

1. **Reading, Comprehension Processes, Grades 2–3**—Relate critical facts and details in narrative or information text to comprehend text.

2. **Reading, Comprehension Processes, Grades 6–8**—Interpret text(s) from multiple perspectives (e.g., historical, cultural, gender, political).

3. **Writing, Rhetoric, Grades 4–5**—Convey meaning, provide important information, make a point, fulfill a purpose.

4. **Writing, Rhetoric, Grades 9–12**—Have an organizing structure that gives the writing coherence (e.g., weaves the threads of meaning into a whole).

5. **Social Studies, Political Science/Civics, Grades K–3**—Create and use surveys, interviews, polls, and/or tallies to find information to solve a real problem or make a decision; for example, create tally sheets to monitor frequency and amount of littering.

6. **Social Studies, Political Science/Civics, Grades 6–8**—Explain and apply tools and methods drawn from political science to examine political issues and/or problems.

7. **Science, Domain I, Inquiry, Grades 4–5**—Design and conduct simple investigations to answer questions or to test ideas about the environment.

8. **Science, Domain I, Inquiry, Grades 9–12**—Communicate and defend scientific explanations and conclusions.

9. **Science, Domain II, Grades K–3**—Explain how sanitary practices, vaccinations, medicines, and other scientific treatments keep people healthy.

10. **Science, Domain II, Grades 6–8**—Describe and exemplify how information and communication technologies affect research and work done in the field of science.

11. **World Languages, Cultures, Grades 4–5**—Identify and use appropriate gestures and other forms of nonverbal communication.

12. **World Languages, Comparisons, Grades 9–12**—Use knowledge of contrasting structural patterns between the target language and the student's own language to communicate effectively.

13. **Music, Singing, Grades K–3**—Sing expressively with appropriate dynamics and phrasing.

14. **Music, Singing, Grades 6–8**—Sing expressively with appropriate dynamics, breath control, phrasing, and nuance, demonstrating understanding of text and style.

Ultimate type of target: 1 = reasoning; 2 = reasoning; 3 = product; 4 = product; 5 = reasoning and product; 6 = knowledge and reasoning; 7 = reasoning and skill; 8 = reasoning and skill or product; 9 = knowledge; 10 = knowledge; 11 = knowledge and skill; 12 = knowledge and reasoning; 13 = skill; 14 = skill

ACTION 3: ENSURE ASSESSMENT QUALITY

Because decisions regarding students are made based on assessment results, it stands to reason that all assessments at classroom, common/interim/benchmark, and annual levels of use should result in dependable information. As stated, many educators lack the background needed to develop, evaluate, and ensure the quality of local assessments—classroom, common, or interim/benchmark. Even evaluating and selecting items from instructional resources or using assessment development tools such as test item banks is problematic without sufficient assessment literacy. As introduced in Part 1, our standards for assessment quality follow, as well as additional detail on each:

- Select a proper assessment method given the learning target to be assessed. Different kinds of achievement (knowledge, reasoning, performance skills, or product development capabilities) align differentially well with the different assessment methods (selected response, written response, performance assessment, and personal communication). Assessment literate educators understand which method to use with which type(s) of learning targets.
- Develop a plan for sampling student achievement using enough exercises to lead to a confident conclusion about student mastery without wasting time gathering too much; that is, know how to get the sharpest focus with greatest efficiency in testing.
- Develop high-quality assessment items, tasks, exercises, and scoring guides for the method selected.
- Understand the sources of bias that can distort assessment results in each context and know what to do to eliminate or minimize that distortion.

How Can You Ensure Assessment Quality?

We've repeated the graphic from Figure 1.1 here (see Figure 2.13) to remind you of our model for quality, and Activity 2.3 (page 51) can assist in understanding the indicators of quality. First, let's briefly examine each key to quality.

Begin with a purpose. Assessment developers cannot build an assessment that will work well unless and until they know who will use the results and how. The purpose of the assessment (formative, assessment *for* learning, or summative) will drive the nature of the results the assessment must yield for its intended purpose and users.

In addition to beginning with a purpose in mind, teachers, or others developing assessments, must also have a clear sense of the specific learning target(s) students are to master. The four types of learning targets with which any curriculum can be classified are knowledge, reasoning, performance skills, and product development targets. The achievement expectations must be reflected both in the assessment method used and in items or tasks that make up the test itself.

With target(s) selected and identified for type of target, developers will then need to manage four design features. First, they must select a proper assessment method for each context. Each of the four assessment methods (selected response, written response, performance assessment, and personal communication) has unique strengths and limitations, and works well in some contexts but not in others. Assessment methods are not interchangeable; the task is to choose a proper method given the target(s) to be

Figure 2.13   Keys to Quality Classroom Assessment

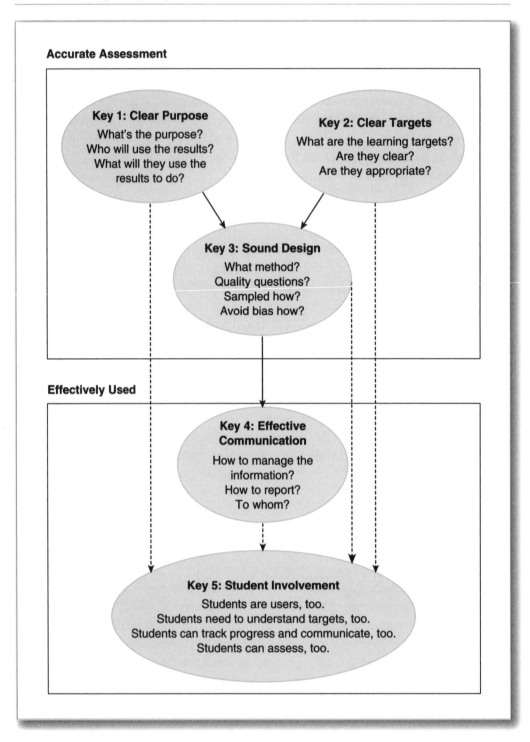

assessed—the quality of any assessment is dependent on this. Figure 2.14 matches achievement targets and assessment methods, noting which combinations make good matches and which do not.

Once assessors have chosen appropriate methods, they then develop a sampling plan. Any assessment is a sample of all the questions one could have posed if the assessment could be infinitely long. Of course, it cannot be, so our task is to create a

Figure 2.14   Matching Assessment Methods to Learning Targets

Target to Be Assessed	Assessment Method			
	Selected Response/Fill-In: Multiple-Choice, True/False, Matching, Fill-In	Written Response	Performance Assessment	Personal Communication
Knowledge	**Good**—can assess isolated elements of knowledge and some relationships among them	**Strong**—can assess elements of knowledge and relationships among them	**Partial**—can assess elements of knowledge and relationships among them in the context of certain tasks	**Strong**—can assess elements of knowledge and relationships among them
Reasoning	**Good**—can assess many, but not all, reasoning targets	**Strong**—can assess all reasoning targets	**Good**—can assess reasoning targets in the context of certain tasks	**Strong**—can assess all reasoning targets
Performance Skill	**Poor**—cannot assess skill level; can only assess prerequisite knowledge and reasoning targets		**Strong**—can observe and assess skills as they are being performed	**Poor**—cannot assess skill level; can only assess prerequisite knowledge and reasoning targets
Product	**Poor**—cannot assess the quality of the product; can only assess prerequisite knowledge and reasoning targets		**Strong**—can directly assess the attributes of quality products	**Poor**—cannot assess the quality of the product; can only assess prerequisite knowledge and reasoning targets

Source: Stiggins, Rick, J.; Chappuis, Jan, *An Introduction to Student-Involved Assessment FOR Learning,* 6th Ed., © 2012, p. 78. Reprinted by permission of Pearson Education, Inc., New York, New York.

representative sample of those questions and, based on the student's success in answering those correctly, we generalize or infer regarding their mastery of the content sampled. We need to include enough items to lead to a confident conclusion. As it turns out, each assessment method brings with it some rules for how to sample with greatest efficiency. One foundation of assessment literacy is to understand those rules of evidence. Our model for sampling (as well as other keys to quality) is drawn from J. Chappuis et al. (2012).

With the sampling plan in mind the next step is the quality assessment exercises (test items/questions, extended written response questions, or performance tasks) and scoring plans such as checklist, rubrics, points awarded for features, and so on. It's just common sense that if the test is to be made up of multiple-choice items, they need to be high-quality items and that the assessment literate developer knows the difference between good and poor items. Similarly, a performance assessment that relies on poor quality scoring rubrics can just as easily lead to scoring inaccuracy and mismeasure learning.

Finally, with respect to assessment quality, every assessment situation brings with it its own list of things that can go wrong and that can distort results—these represent sources of bias. For instance, a score on any assessment can misrepresent a student's real achievement if the assessment environment is distracting, the directions are misleading, the student suffers from extreme test anxiety, or subjective scoring procedures for extended response or performance assessments are ignored or conducted by untrained raters. To prevent this we only need understand the potential sources of distortion due to bias in their particular context. The ideal is that every assessor can anticipate what can go wrong in various assessment contexts and prevent those problems when possible. Bias can arise from the quality or nature of the assessment itself, the fit of that assessment into the culture of the classroom, the environment within which the assessment is conducted, or the relationship between the assessment and the instruction provided leading up to it. The point is those sources generally are known and remedies are available for most of them.

Figure 2.15 can assist teachers and administrators in applying the keys to quality to their assessment system. The left column identifies each key; the column to the right translates the key into specific teacher classroom assessment competencies.

Figure 2.15   Indicators of Sound Classroom Assessment Practice

1. **Why Assess?** Assessment Processes and Results Serve Clear and Appropriate Purposes	a. Teachers understand who the users and uses of classroom assessment information are and know their information needs.
	b. Teachers understand the relationship between assessment and student motivation and craft assessment experiences to maximize motivation.
	c. Teachers use classroom assessment processes and results formatively (assessment *for* learning).
	d. Teachers use classroom assessment results summatively (assessment *of* learning) to inform someone beyond the classroom about students' achievement as of a particular point in time.
	e. Teachers have a comprehensive plan over time for integrating assessment *for* and *of* learning in the classroom.
2. **Assess What?** Assessments Reflect Clear and Valued Student Learning Targets	a. Teachers have clear learning targets for students; they know how to turn broad statements of content standards into classroom-level targets.
	b. Teachers understand the various types of learning targets they hold for students.
	c. Teachers select learning targets focused on the most important things students need to know and be able to do.
	d. Teachers have a comprehensive plan over time for assessing learning targets.
3. **Assess How?** Learning Targets Are Translated Into Assessments That Yield Accurate Results	a. Teachers understand what the various assessment methods are.
	b. Teachers choose assessment methods that match intended learning targets.
	c. Teachers design assessments that serve intended purposes.
	d. Teachers sample learning appropriately in their assessments.
	e. Teachers write assessment questions of all types well.
	f. Teachers avoid sources of bias that distort results.

4. **Communicate How?** Assessment Results Are Managed Well and Communicated Effectively	a. Teachers record assessment information accurately, keep it confidential, and appropriately combine and summarize it for reporting (including grades). Such summary accurately reflects current level of student learning.
	b. Teachers select the best reporting option (grades, narratives, portfolios, conferences) for each context (learning targets and users).
	c. Teachers interpret and use standardized test results correctly.
	d. Teachers effectively communicate assessment results to students.
	e. Teachers effectively communicate assessment results to a variety of audiences outside the classroom, including parents, colleagues, and other stakeholders.
5. **Involve Students How?** Students Are Involved in Their Own Assessment	a. Teachers make learning targets clear to students.
	b. Teachers involve students in assessing, tracking, and setting goals for their own learning.
	c. Teachers involve students in communicating about their own learning.

Source: Chappuis, Jan; Stiggins, Rick J.; Chappuis, Steve; Arter, Judith A., *Classroom Assessment* for *Student Learning: Doing It Right—Using It Well*, 2nd Ed., © 2012, pp. 27, 64. Reprinted by permission of Pearson Education, Inc., New York, New York.

Note: Sound classroom assessment practice = Skill in gathering accurate information + Effective use of information and procedures

ACTIVITY 2.3

Indicators of Sound Classroom Assessment Practice

PURPOSE

Figure 2.15 presents a set of indicators of teacher competence for each of the five keys to quality classroom assessment: clear and appropriate purposes, clear and appropriate targets, sound design, effective communication, and student involvement. The indicators can be used in at least two ways:

1. Leaders can use them to as a basis for discussing with teachers their understanding and use of quality classroom assessments.

2. Teachers can use them to self-assess their own understanding of quality standards for assessment.

TIME

1 hour for the main activity

MATERIALS NEEDED

- Flip charts, markers, and easels if available
- Interactive whiteboard or computer with projection if available to assist with recording and viewing work
- Copies of the list of indicators (Figure 2.15)

SUGGESTED ROOM SETUP

- Tables and chairs for small groups to work together
- Space to post the charts around the room for a gallery walk

DIRECTIONS

Read through the indicators (Figure 2.15). Then divide into pairs or small groups and assign each group one of the five keys to quality classroom assessment. Each group brainstorms what strong and weak classroom performance would look like for each indicator and writes them on chart paper. Groups then do a gallery tour—post the charts around the room and everyone walks around, reading each group's responses. Finally, the whole group discusses how you might use the keys, indicators, and performance continua to promote teacher development in this arena.

 Available for download at **http://www.resources.corwin.com/ChappuisBalancedAssessment**

ACTION 4: BUILD EFFECTIVE SYSTEMS FOR COMMUNICATING ASSESSMENT RESULTS

Most learners welcome the kind of feedback that helps them understand how to improve, and student growth can be sustained with effective feedback. But students also need to know and understand that, ultimately, they will be held accountable for meeting certain learning expectations. Both forms of feedback, descriptive and evaluative, done well can serve valuable purposes. But they both need to be backed up with effective communication of results designed to serve the purpose of the assessment. So effective communication is different in its form when intending to support learning versus to report a judgment of that learning. Balanced assessment systems accommodate these differences.

While students are learning when formative assessment and assessment *for* learning are in play, the feedback students receive will encourage and support student learning when it does the following:

- Focuses on attributes of the student's work rather than attributes of the student as a learner ("here is how to make your writing more effective" rather than "just try harder")
- Is descriptive of that work, revealing to the student how to do better the next time rather than judgmental
- Is clearly understood by the intended user, leading to specific inferences about what is needed
- Is sufficiently detailed to be helpful yet not so comprehensive as to overwhelm
- Arrives in time to inform the learning (Hattie & Timperely, 2007)

Other researchers and thought leaders tells us that feedback that supports student learning—that is, helps them learn more—does the following:

- Points out successes and gives specific information about how to improve the performance or product (Black, Harrison, Lee, Marshall, & Wiliam, 2002; Black & Wiliam, 1998)
- Offers information about progress relative to the intended learning goal and about what action to take to reach the goal (Hattie & Timperley, 2007)
- Directs comments to the quality of the work—what was done well and what needs improving—increasing student interest in the task and level of achievement (Butler, 1988)
- Emphasizes learning goals, which leads to greater learning gains than feedback that emphasizes self-esteem (Ames, 1992; Butler, 1988; Hattie & Timperley, 2007)
- Cues the individual to direct attention to the *quality of the task* rather than to *self* (praise, effort, etc.), which appears to have a negative effect on learning; many studies speak to effective teachers praising less than average (Cameron & Pierce, 1994; Kluger & DeNisi, 1996)
- Addresses partial understanding; when student work demonstrates lack of understanding, feedback will not help (Hattie & Timperley, 2007)

This places classroom teachers at the center of good communication, because they are in position to not only deliver but also to maximize the quality and effective use of this kind of feedback.

On the summative or evaluative side, when reporting student learning for accountability purposes, such as a report card, the following attributes are important:

- The data or information underpinning the communication must be accurate—inaccurate assessment leads to miscommunication about student learning. Put another way, the results (which include the scores and grades) of any assessment are only as good as the assessment itself.
- Both the message sender (teacher, school, district, test report, etc.) and receiver (students, parents, community) must understand the achievement target in question to be the same thing—where there is misalignment there will be miscommunication. If classroom, interim, and annual assessments are all not based on the same set of standards this is bound to happen. But this is also where student- and parent-friendly versions of the learning targets can help. If the learning target(s) are clear to all involved from the beginning of instruction and assessment a strong foundation for good communication is put in place.
- If symbols (such as grades or test scores) used to communicate the evaluative judgment about each student's achievement status are understood by all involved to mean the same thing then effective communication is possible. But if they think the scores, symbols, or grades mean different things, they will miscommunicate.

Although much progress has been made in the area of schools transitioning to standards-based report cards, we know that many parents are still conditioned to traditional communication models. Secondary schools in particular feel the need to deliver traditional grades and GPAs and rank in class because of the demands of higher education, scholarship awards, and so on. But when parents see dozens of marks in a teacher's grade book it is easy for them to confuse quantity with the quality of a grade. Communication about student progress to them that is formative in nature doesn't reflect their own school experience, meaning leaders and teachers will need to take extra time and care in helping parents understand the role of both kinds of feedback. When parents understand the shift in focus from teaching to learning, and see the effects of the use of descriptive feedback with their children, they will understand the need no longer exists to put a grade on everything the student does. We explore more about sound grading practices in Part 3.

ACTION 5: LINK ASSESSMENT TO STUDENT MOTIVATION WITH ASSESSMENT *FOR* LEARNING STRATEGIES

If we accept that part of the new school mission is to promote academic success for all learners, then the emotional dynamics of the assessment experience become important to keep in the forefront. We can adopt teaching and assessment practices that keep all students believing that success is achievable if they strive for it. With that frame of mind, regardless of the level of their performance they attain on an assessment, they can say to themselves, "I understand these results. I know what to do next, and I choose to keep trying." The pessimistic perspective to be avoided brings a student to conclude that "I have no idea what this means or what to do about it. I'm not good at this anyway. I quit." This kind of hopelessness stops learning. Formative assessment *for* learning strategies can help teachers bring all students to the optimistic side of learning.

Balanced assessment systems accomplish this when they include the student as a significant decision maker, whose information needs must be met. We can incorporate formative assessment practices into our teaching that keep students in touch with the answers to these three guiding questions (Sadler, 1989):

- What am I trying to learn?
- Where am in now in relation to that target?
- How can I close the gap between where I am now and where I need to be?

We believe the key to creating and sustaining student motivation is to use the classroom assessment process *during the learning* to help them see their gaps narrowing. The intent is to involve them in continuous self-monitoring so that they become aware of and come to feel in control of their own growth; it is to bring them to a place where they can say to themselves, "I'm not there yet, but I know where there is, and I am getting closer. I can do this!" Fear and anxiety are replaced with confidence and persistence.

Note that the locus of assessment control in the three questions above resides with the student. Sadler (1989) identifies student involvement in assessment during their learning as of paramount importance: "The indispensable conditions for improvement are that the *student* comes to hold a concept of quality roughly similar to that held by the teacher, is able to monitor continuously the quality of what is being produced *during the act of production itself*, and has a repertoire of alternative moves or strategies from which to draw at any given point" (p. 121, emphasis in original).

In his research in the domain of learned helplessness, Seligman (1998) states that optimism matters as much as talent or desire when it comes to success. Those with an optimistic outlook see themselves as having personal control over their lives and over their decision making. When they experience defeat, they do not interpret it as a personal indictment of their capabilities but, rather, as an indication that they did not use the right strategy or did not put forth enough effort at the time. For them the goal is still attainable, and they know that they are capable of improving. They feel in control of the situation.

On the other hand, those with a pessimistic outlook who experience success might interpret it as a fluke. When they meet defeat, they believe that they failed because they are not capable. For them, defeat is habitual; in other words, they interpret it as personal, pervasive, and permanent. They do not see their actions paying off and feel a lack of control and a sense of helplessness.

Both sets of behaviors are learned. Teachers can help students see that they have the ability to change situations by their own, deliberate actions, and the consistent application of quality classroom assessment practices used to support learning can help promote this.

Assessment *for* Learning: Bringing Students Onboard

After completing a comprehensive review of research on formative assessment practices in 1998, British researchers Paul Black and Dylan Wiliam reported that these practices consistently led to significant increases in student achievement: The gains they noted were among the largest reported for any instructional intervention. In summarizing their findings, they concluded the following practices had the highest impact on student growth in achievement:

- Use of evidence gathered during classroom discussions, classroom work, and homework to determine current state of student understanding, with action taken to improve learning and correct misunderstandings
- Provision of feedback during the learning, with guidance on how to improve
- Development of student self-assessment and peer-feedback skills

Formative assessment practices not only keep teachers in touch with student learning, they also keep students in touch with their progress, which helps develop their own understanding that their actions can make a difference in their achievement. Jan Chappuis (2015) offers seven assessment *for* learning strategies focused on the needs of the learner. This instructional framework helps maximize both motivation and achievement by involving students from the start in their own learning and assessment.

To help students understand where they are going:

Strategy 1: Provide Students with a Clear and Understandable Vision of the Learning Target. Motivation and achievement both increase when instruction is guided by clearly defined targets. Activities that help students answer the question, "What's the learning?" set the stage for all further formative assessment actions. Share learning targets in language students understand. Connect daily activities with these targets by asking, "Why are we doing this activity?" and "What are we learning?"

Also, ask students to consider what constitutes quality in a product or performance and then show how their thoughts match with the rubric you will use to define quality. Provide students with rubrics written in student-friendly language or develop scoring criteria with them.

Strategy 2: Use Examples and Models of Strong and Weak Work. Carefully chosen examples and nonexamples can create and refine students' understanding of the learning goal by helping students answer the questions, "What defines quality work?" and "What are some problems to avoid?" Use models of strong and weak work—anonymous student work, work from life beyond school, and your own work. Begin with work that demonstrates strengths and weaknesses related to problems students commonly experience, especially the problems that most concern you. Students analyze these anonymous samples for quality and then justify their judgments. When you engage students in analyzing examples or models, they will be developing a vision of what the product or performance looks like when it's done well. They will also be rehearsing for eventual self-assessment.

To help them know where they are now in relation to expectations:

Strategy 3: Offer Regular Descriptive Feedback During the Learning. Effective feedback shows students where they are on their path to attaining the intended learning. It answers for students the questions, "What are my strengths?"; "What do I need to work on?"; and "Where did I go wrong, and what can I do about it?" Offer descriptive feedback instead of grades on work that is for practice. This feedback should reflect student strengths and areas for improvement with respect to the specific learning target(s) they are trying to hit in a given assignment. Feedback is most effective when it identifies what students are doing right, as well as what they need to work on next. What did learners accomplish? What are the next steps? All learners, especially struggling ones, need to know that they did something right, and your job is to find it and label it for them before launching into what they need to improve.

Learners don't need to know everything that needs correcting all at once. Narrow your comments to the specific knowledge and skills emphasized in the current assignment and pay attention to how much feedback learners can act on at one time. Students will not be harmed if you don't point out all their problems. Identify as many issues as students can successfully act on at one time, independently, and then figure out what to teach next based on the other problems in their work. Providing students with descriptive feedback is a crucial part of increasing achievement. Additionally, we can prepare students to offer each other feedback though deliberate use of Strategies 1 and 2.

Strategy 4: Teach Students to Self-Assess and Set Goals for Next Steps. The information provided in effective feedback models the kind of thinking we want students to be able to do about their own work. Strategy 4 teaches them to identify their strengths and weaknesses and to set goals for further learning. It involves having them answer the questions, "What am I good at?"; "What do I need to work on?"; and "What should I do next?"

Self-assessment is proven contributor to increased learning and a necessary part of becoming a self-regulated learner. It is not an add-on if you have the time or the *right* students. Struggling students are as much the right students as any others. Monitoring and regulating their own learning can be taught to all kinds of students, including those with learning disabilities (Andrade, 2010). To be accurate self-assessors, students need a clear vision of the intended learning, practice with identifying strengths and weaknesses in a variety of examples, and experience with acting on feedback that models *self-assessment* thinking: "What have I done well? Where do I need to continue working?"

To help students close the gap between
where they are now and where they want to be:

Strategy 5: Use Evidence of Student Learning Needs to Determine Next Steps in Teaching. With this strategy, we use diagnostic assessment information, gathered formally or informally, to plan next steps in instruction. We make sure that our diagnostic assessments have *instructional traction*: that they help identify the type of learning needs underlying mistakes. We analyze mistakes to determine the cause—incomplete understanding, flaws in reasoning, or misconceptions—and then plan instruction to address the type of learning need.

While Strategies 1 through 4 offer a progression of activities, Strategy 5 can occur at any time—before, during, or after instruction.

Strategy 6: Design Focused Instruction, Followed by Practice With Feedback. Strategy 5 is only worth doing if we plan time in the instructional sequence to do something with the resulting information. Strategy 6 scaffolds learning by narrowing the focus of a lesson to address specific problems identified in Strategy 5. When a concept, skill, or competence proves difficult for students, we can provide further instruction and then let them practice, offering feedback on just the aspects they are practicing, prior to reassessing for a grade. This narrows the volume of corrective feedback students, especially struggling students, need to attend to at a given time and raises their chances of success at doing so. It is a time saver for you and more instructionally powerful for your students.

Strategy 7: Provide Opportunities for Students to Track, Reflect on, and Share Their Learning Progress. Long-term retention and motivation increase when students track, reflect on, and communicate about their learning. Any activity that requires students to look back on their journey and share their achievement with others both reinforces the learning and helps them develop insights into themselves as learners. These kinds of activities give students the opportunity to notice their own strengths, to see how far they have come, and to feel in control of the conditions of their success. By reflecting on their learning, they deepen their understanding and will remember it longer. In addition, it is the learner, not the teacher, who is doing the work.

ACTIVITY 2.4

Assessment for Learning Self-Evaluation

PURPOSE

To offer teachers an opportunity to think about where they are now with respect to key assessment *for* learning practices.

TIME

25–30 minutes

MATERIALS NEEDED

- A copy of the handout "Assessment *for* Learning Self-Evaluation" for each participant, shown in Figure 2.16
- The numbers 1 to 5 each written on a separate 8-1/2 × 11–inch piece of paper (for posting on the wall)
- The graphing chart reproduced as a large poster
- A fat-tip marker (1/2 to 3/4 inch)

SUGGESTED ROOM SETUP

- Tables for participants' independent work (Directions Item 1)
- Open wall space with the numbers 1 to 5 posted about six feet high and three to five feet apart so that people will be able to see them when lined up (Directions Items 2 and 3)

DIRECTIONS

1. Ask participants to number from 1 to 6 on a separate piece of paper. Tell them not to put their names on it—this activity will be anonymous. Then have them evaluate their own classroom practice for each of the six statements on the survey "Assessment *for* Learning Self-Evaluation" (see Figure 2.16) using the scale of 1 to 5 as described on the survey. This usually takes about 5 minutes.

Figure 2.16   Assessment *for* Learning Self-Evaluation

On a separate piece of paper, number from 1 to 6.

Rate your current classroom practice for each of the six statements by using the following scale:

1 = I don't do this, or this doesn't happen in my classroom.

2 = I do this infrequently, or this happens infrequently in my classroom.

3 = I do this sometimes, or this sometimes happens in my classroom.

4 = I do this frequently, or this happens frequently in my classroom.

5 = I do this on an ongoing basis, or this happens all the time in my classroom.

Survey Statements

1. I communicate learning targets to students in language they can understand, as a regular part of instruction.
2. I use examples and models to help students understand key elements of a quality response, product, or performance.
3. I offer feedback that links directly to the intended learning, pointing out strengths and offering information to guide improvement. Students receive this feedback during the learning process, with opportunities to improve on each learning target before the graded event.
4. I design assignments and assessments so that students can self-assess, by identifying their own strengths and areas for further study regarding intended learning. The results of assignments and assessments function as effective feedback to students.
5. I use assessment information to focus instruction day to day in the classroom.
6. I give students regular opportunities to track, reflect on, and share their achievement status and improvement.

2. After everyone has finished, have participants wad their papers into snowballs, move to the open area, and form a circle. Ask them to throw their snowballs at each other, picking one up and throwing it to someone else two or three times. This usually takes about 5 minutes.

3. Ask everyone to find a snowball, open the paper up and "be" that person. They should find the rating next to Statement 1 (it will be a number from 1 to 5), and line up in front of the appropriate number you have posted on the wall. Ask the person at the head of each line to count the people. Graph the number of people standing in each line on the chart, using a blown-up version of Figure 2.17 and a big marking pen. Then read the statement aloud. Do the same for each of the remaining statements. This usually takes about 10 minutes.

4. Debrief by asking participants to find a partner and comment on the results they see charted and implications for further learning. Then conduct a large-group discussion of observations. This usually takes 5 to 10 minutes.

Figure 2.17   Assessment *for* Learning Self-Evaluation Results Graph

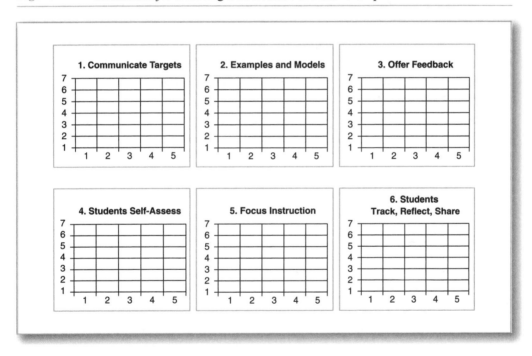

 Available for download at **http://www.resources.corwin.com/ChappuisBalancedAssessment**

THINKING ABOUT ASSESSMENT: SUPPORT RESOURCES FOR PART 2

The following resource that relates directly to the content presented in Part 2 is intended to either deepen understanding or assist leaders in implementing a balanced assessment system.

ACTIVITY 2.5

Local Assessment System Self-Evaluation

We have transformed to five actions described above into of 5-point rating scales (see Figure 2.18). Each scale represents a continuum of development for an action. We provide this as a summary of key ideas on Part 2 and as the basis for you to conduct a self-evaluation of the current status of your district for each.

Read through the items in the District Assessment System Self-Evaluation for each of the five actions. Discuss each item within your team and come to agreement about where you would place your school/district along the item's accompanying 5-point rating scale. Consider the following prior to completing the activity:

- The larger, more diverse team you can assemble that is representative of your school/district, the more accurate your profile is likely to be. Or your team can do the profiling activity first and then repeat it with a larger group to create more understanding of the issues and gain a larger representation of opinion.
- If a larger district or school team is assembled, coming to consensus about each item may be more difficult because people will bring not only different perspectives but also very different realities. For example, one person's school may deserve a high rating on one action while another school in the district hasn't even considered that scope of work and therefore admittedly gets a lower mark. How can that be reconciled to reflect the work the district needs to accomplish? Or the district may be doing well overall in one area but that work has not filtered into the schools. How should the team rate the district overall?
- What one knows and doesn't know when asked to make judgments or evaluations influences one's answers to questions. In this activity—as in many others in this guide—participants' responses are directly related to their level of assessment literacy.

Figure 2.18   School/District Assessment System Self-Evaluation

Action 1: Balance Your Assessment System

Definition: Balanced assessment systems serve different users at different levels of assessment by providing them all with the information they need to fulfill their responsibilities. Such a system balances effective assessment use at the classroom level with interim/benchmark assessment and annual accountability assessment to serve both formative and summative purposes. This action advocates examination of current levels of balance and movement toward greater balance if needed.

5 Implemented	4	3 Progressing	2	1 Getting Started
All faculty and staff are aware of differences in assessment purpose across classroom, common, interim/benchmark, and annual level and know how to use each to support and to verify student learning.		There is inconsistency among the staff with how we use assessments to improve our school; we are aware of the need for balance and have begun to plan for balanced assessment.		There is little awareness in the district of differences in purpose, assessment users, or assessment uses across classroom, interim and annual levels of use.

Our highest assessment priority is to help students develop the capacity and disposition to assess their own achievement and to use their assessment results to improve their own learning.	Faculty and staff recognize that students are important assessment users who make data-based instructional decisions that impact their own success and have made some progress in helping them do so.	Students have not been regarded as key assessment users, and there is little awareness (or support) of the need to bring them into the assessment process.
We have an assessment system in place that is meeting the information needs of classroom, interim, and annual assessment users.	We have an plan we are working on and have begun to design this balanced system	As yet no such system has been conceived, designed, or developed.
We have an information management system in place to collect, house, and deliver achievement information to the intended users at classroom, interim, and annual assessment levels.	We have an tentative plan in place and have begun to investigate available information management systems for this use.	As yet no such system has been conceived, designed, developed, or purchased.
Our school board and community are aware of the need for balanced assessment and are supportive of this priority.	We are currently educating our staff, policy makers, and community of the need to development an assessment system to meet diverse information needs across levels.	Our policy makers and community are unaware of the need to think of assessment in this manner.

Action 2: Continue to Refine Achievement Standards

Definition: It is not possible to dependably assess achievement targets unless they have been completely defined; that is, clear learning targets are needed to underpin all levels of assessment. This action calls for the development of clear targets as a foundation for balanced assessment.

5 Implemented	4	3 Progressing	2	1 Getting Started
We have reviewed and refined our local achievement standards to align with state/CCSS standards and to represent our highest priority learning outcomes.		We are aware of the need for us to refine and make clear our own academic standards and are in the process of doing so.		We have only adopted state standards or are using externally developed curriculum.
Our curriculum presents learning progressions in which our expectations unfold over time within and across grade levels in a manner consistent with state standards and the way learning unfolds.		We are developing our grade-level and subject-area maps in the form of progressions that link learning prerequisites throughout the learning.		We have grade level standards, but they are not articulated or connected with one another in a unified manner.
We have deconstructed each of our priority standards into the scaffolding necessary for clarity; that is, we know the foundations of knowledge, reasoning, performance skills, and product development capabilities at each subject and grade level that build to success.		We are in the process of deconstructing each of our standards into the scaffolding leading to competence.		The deconstruction process has not been initiated.

(Continued)

(Continued)

We have further refined standards into learning targets that will guide daily classroom instruction and assessment and have developed student- and family-friendly versions to share with stakeholders as appropriate.	We are in the process of making those changes and additions.	This transformation process has yet to be initiated.
We have verified that each teacher in each classroom is a master of the achievement standards that their students are expected to master.	We have identified contexts in which professional development is needed to assure teacher competence regarding content area knowledge.	There has been little or no investigation of teacher preparedness in their own content area(s).

Action 3: Ensure Assessment Quality

Definition: Because many decisions are made based on assessment results, it is necessary that all assessments at classroom, interim, and annual levels of use yield dependable information about student achievement. This action asks for the evaluation of all current assessments to verify quality.

5 Implemented	4	3 Progressing	2	1 Getting Started
We have established and understand the criteria by which we should judge the quality of our assessments.		We are aware of the need for standards of assessment quality upon which to evaluate our work and are working to establish our criteria.		No such criteria have been identified; no quality control framework exists for us at any level.
We have conducted the professional development needed to learn to use those assessment quality criteria in a consistent manner.		We have a plan in place for conducting that training process to prepare us to evaluate the quality of our assessments.		No such professional development has been conducted.
We have conducted (and regularly conduct) a local evaluation(s) on the quality of our assessments.		We are aware of the need to conduct such an evaluation and are planning to conduct it.		There is no awareness of the need for or plans to conduct such an evaluation.
As a result of our evaluation for quality, we know that the level of assessments quality throughout our systems and implemented plans for them all to be of high quality.		We have found that our assessments vary in quality across contexts but we know where the inadequacies and gaps are.		The quality of our assessments may be poor—we haven't checked.

Action 4: Build Effective Systems for Communicating Assessment Results

Definition: When feedback to students takes certain forms and is delivered in certain ways, it can positively impact student confidence, motivation, and achievement. This action asks that feedback delivered to students satisfy the conditions necessary to make that happen.

5 Implemented	4	3 Progressing	2	1 Getting Started
We understand and embrace the characteristics of feedback that permits it to support learning or to certify it accurately when that is the purpose.		We are starting to understand the role descriptive feedback can play in helping students learn but have not taken systemic action to ensure it is present in every classroom.		The feedback we provide is in the form of grades and test scores that judge or evaluate student achievement.

We have completed the professional development needed to understand and implement classroom communication strategies that support student learning and have provided training in sound grading practices.	We plan to offer or are in the process of conducting the professional development needed to balance evaluative and descriptive feedback.	No such professional development has yet been considered or implemented.
In our classrooms, we a balance the use of descriptive feedback that supports learning and evaluative feedback (e.g., grades).	Our teachers are starting to use descriptive feedback during student practice to help students improve before they are to be held accountable for their learning.	Evaluative feedback is the predominate form of communication in our classrooms.

Action 5: Link Assessment to Student Motivation With Assessment *for* Learning Strategies

Definition: The common practice of relying on the anxiety and intimidation of accountability to motivate learning works for some students. It can energize those who have hope of success. But for students who have experienced chronic failure, anxiety can drive them further away from a desire to learn or a belief they can succeed. For them, success at learning is the motivation they need. This action urges educators to embrace the emotional dynamics: the link between assessment and student motivation.

5 Implemented	4	3 Progressing	2	1 Getting Started
Our faculty, staff, leaders, policy makers, and community all support the use of student-involved assessment to help all students experience the kind of academic success needed to remain confident and engaged.		We are in the process of helping all stakeholders understand and embrace the power of student-involved assessment during their learning.		We motivate students largely by holding them accountable for learning.
We have conducted the professional development needed to build our capacity and dispositions needed to use assessment *for* learning to motivate all students to strive for success.		That professional development is planned or underway that will result in the development of capacity and dispositions throughout the faculty.		As yet no such professional development has been considered or offered.
The classroom assessment practices we use rely heavily on student involvement in assessment during their learning to maintain their confidence and motivation.		The proportion of our teachers who involve their students in ongoing self-assessment as a motivator is increasingly steadily.		Our classroom practices rarely include student-involved assessment practices.

 Available for download at **http://www.resources.corwin.com/ChappuisBalancedAssessment**

Individual Leadership Actions for Balance and Quality

We know two of the school-related factors that positively influence student learning are classroom instruction and school leadership. And as noted in the Interstate School Leaders Licensure Consortium (ISLLC) standards, leaders have the greatest impact when they have a clear vision and set direction with aligned goals and purposes, serving to strengthen and solidify the faculty (Council of Chief State School Officers, 2008).

Given that, in Part 3 we continue to focus largely on supporting the classroom level of assessment in a balanced system. In addition to the difference in student achievement that effective school leaders can make, there are two other reasons we keep our focus on assessment leadership for the classroom.

First, standards-driven instruction has created new knowledge requirements and responsibilities for school leaders. In today's systems, the practice of sorting students along a bell curve, thereby artificially creating winners and losers, is being replaced by a mission that *all* students must learn well. Instead of a curriculum driven by textbooks and focused on what teachers should teach, standards identify what students should know and be able to do. These standards are public and communicate what a state or district values and expects in student learning. Assessing the standards, not just through large-scale annual accountability tests or even local interim assessments but also day to day in the classroom, where standards, instruction, and assessment can all be pages in the same book, is now a must to fully prepare students for academic success. So separating the schools we grew up in from the schools we desire and changing the underlying beliefs and conditions for that transition is clearly a leadership challenge.

The second reason is the reward of improved student learning brought about by the use of classroom formative assessment, or assessment *for* learning. Summarized by Black and Wiliam (1998) and described by Fullan (2004) as "a high-yield strategy," the research reported on the topic helps explain why leadership knowledge specific to that area of classroom assessment is beneficial.

In Part 1, we described a framework for a balanced system. In Part 2, we described five organizational actions that help put that system in place. We asked you to analyze your organization relative to each action and provided considerations and suggestions for implementation. In Part 3, we turn our attention to leadership actions that *individual* leaders at the school and district level can take to personally support assessment balance and quality. There are many other ways to work toward implementing the five organizational actions—we provide only a start.

As you move through these actions, keeping in mind a conceptual framework that puts them in a context beyond just supporting the five organizational actions may be of help. Much of what leaders do falls into three areas. The leader

1. establishes and communicates a vision,

2. provides the necessary resources, and

3. works at removing the barriers that stand in the way of achieving the vision.

The leadership actions needed to get to a balanced, quality assessment system may require improvement of what is already occurring or may require the organization do something entirely new. Both a mindset of improvement and one of innovation will be helpful in building an assessment system based on quality and balance (Davidovich, Nikolay, Laugerman, & Commodore, 2010).

INDIVIDUAL LEADERSHIP ACTIONS

1. Deepen your personal understanding of a sound and balanced assessment system and the conditions required to achieve it.

2. Promote the necessity and use of clear academic achievement standards in every subject and grade level with aligned classroom-level learning targets and the understanding of their relationship to the development of accurate assessments.

3. Promote and communicate standards of quality for student assessments, helping teachers learn to assess accurately, and work to ensure that these standards are met in all school/district assessments. This includes ensuring the assessment literacy of teacher teams developing assessments for use across grade levels or subject areas.

4. Deepen your knowledge of formative assessment practices that involve students and work with staff to integrate them into classroom instruction.

5. Create the conditions necessary for the appropriate use and reporting of student achievement information, including report card grades.

6. Form or participate in peer learning groups to practice observing and evaluating teacher classroom assessment competencies.

7. Review and examine current school/district assessment-related policies for alignment to sound assessment practice, and encourage revision as needed.

INDIVIDUAL LEADERSHIP ACTION 1: Deepen your personal understanding of a sound and balanced assessment system and the conditions required to achieve it.

Assessment-literate school leaders can help bring balance and quality to their local assessment system through their everyday role and responsibilities in instructional leadership. In a nutshell, they seek opportunities to bring balance at all levels of assessment to the following:

- Assessment purpose
- Achievement targets
- Assessment methods
- Communication methods

In seeking to balance assessment *purpose*, it distills down to balancing summative assessments, those that check achievement status at a given point in time, including both classroom status checks and those conducted using standardized tests, with formative assessments, including classroom assessments *for* learning. These are assessments specifically designed to involve students in the assessment process, to provide practice, and to inform them about their own progress. Each level and type of assessment requires its own support resources, professional development, and integration into school improvement.

Second, leaders look for a balance of achievement *targets*. If the grade level or course curriculum derived from state standards, or if the classroom curriculum comes from other sources, and either predominantly reflects knowledge targets at the expense of more complex reasoning, skill, and product targets, an imbalance in what students learn results.

Third, they monitor balance of assessment *methods* (selected response, written response, performance assessment, and personal communication), achieved in part through a proper balance of learning targets in the written curriculum. Assuming the curriculum standards do have an appropriate mix of knowledge, reasoning, skill, and product targets, if students getting a steady diet of selected response assessments using optical marks scanners it's a pretty safe bet that some of those standards are not being assessed well, or at all. The opposite of that scenario: We knew a middle school science teacher who for many years used only performance assessment to assess her students. After some assessment literacy training, she understood that many of the knowledge targets, the building blocks of science, were getting assessed either poorly or inefficiently, or both.

Fourth, they ensure a balance of *communication* methods, which allows students, parents, and other stakeholders to gain access to timely and understandable information about student achievement. At the classroom level, beyond test marks and report card grades, this could include providing regular descriptive feedback to students, allowing students to self-assess and peer assess, holding student-led conferences to allow students to share what they know and their own progress, and providing still other opportunities for students to communicate about their own learning.

Some of the activities in this book are meant to extend understanding, while others can guide direct action. If you have not conducted a school/district assessment audit (see Activity 2.1), completing this activity can form the foundation of *next steps* in getting to balance and quality.

ACTIVITY 3.1

Merging Local and State Assessment Systems

PURPOSE

We've advocated that a local assessment program function as a system, with each component sharing a clear purpose, all working toward the same goal of improved student learning. This activity extends the systems-thinking approach to assessment by asking participants to consider what is necessary to achieve a level of balance and synergy between a state system and a local assessment system.

TIME

1 hour

MATERIALS NEEDED

- The grids from the assessment audit of your school/district in Activity 2.1
- Information on your state assessment(s)—test and item specifications, test examples or methods, sample reports distributed at the district, school, teacher, and student levels

SUGGESTED ROOM SETUP

- Tables and chairs set for ease of discussion among participants
- Interactive whiteboards or easels with flip charts and markers to record discussion and decision making

DIRECTIONS

First, you will need to have completed the assessment audit in Activity 2.1 in Part 2. This activity helped map the big picture of assessment in your school or district. In addition, gather information about the state assessment system, including test and item specifications, released samples of the various assessments, methods used, online resources, professional development provided, and sample reports from state assessments to the various levels: district, school, teacher, and student. If your state is using the Common Core State Standards (CCSS), much of this information can be obtained from the two testing consortia. Remember that it is difficult for any single test to deliver accurate, reliable, and meaningful information if the test is spread too thinly among multiple purposes. With this information, consider the following questions:

- What is (are) the purpose(s) of the state test(s)?
- Considering your big picture, what specific summative (accountability) decisions need to be made based on assessment results, and who is making them?
- Of these, which can be informed by state assessment results? Which cannot?
- What formative uses (supporting student learning) need to be informed by assessment results? Who is making those decisions?
- Which of these can and cannot be informed by state assessment results?

Now go back to the big picture of assessment in your school/district once again in relation to your answers to the above questions.

- If there are information needs the state tests do not meet, are they being met currently by district, school, or classroom assessments?
- Are there subjects that seem over-tested while others are not tested at all?
- Is there redundancy among state, district, and school assessments?
- What information should your local assessment system provide? To whom? For what purposes?

And possibly most important, are all assessments at every level based on the learning targets found in the state standards? If the adopted and written curriculum is not always the tested curriculum what needs to happen to get the system in sync?

CLOSURE

Answers to the questions above can guide your choices of what to test locally and how to test it.

No doubt your team could pose other questions about how to get the most from a system that integrates state and local assessment. You might address balance in standards or targets tested, assessment methods used, or methods for communicating the information to the users. You could also look at balance from the summative/formative perspective; are students getting opportunities to practice before having to show what they know for an accountability purpose? Our purpose in this activity is to illustrate the opportunity local leaders have to improve balance and quality, even if the state system might drive the majority of public focus and attention.

 Available for download at **http://www.resources.corwin.com/ChappuisBalancedAssessment**

INDIVIDUAL LEADERSHIP ACTION 2:
Promote the necessity and use of clear academic achievement standards in every subject and grade level with aligned classroom-level learning targets and the understanding of their relationship to the development of accurate assessments.

Many students come to school every day prepared to learn, yet are not always given a clear sense of what is being asked of them. Those who cannot clearly see the target will have difficulty hitting it. Students can succeed when they know what they are expected to achieve. But many teachers are still adrift in a sea of standards; they may have CCSS or other state standards, supporting curriculum frameworks, grade-level and subject-area documents, and curriculum guides aligning standards to textbook material, not to mention the adopted texts and supplemental materials themselves. Without the training, support, and time needed to transfer it all into everyday lessons, the priority standards for each grade level and each subject may be swamped by the amount of competing and unaligned content available.

So it seems fair to assume that if the curriculum floor of the house is in disarray, then the assessment floor is going to be equally messy. As we have stated, the fact that most districts already have a set of standards and supportive written curriculum may or may not be enough. This action for individual school leaders asks that they ensure that classroom instruction aims directly at the written curriculum, that learning targets are at a level of specificity and clarity for lesson planning, and that the targets are made clear to all stakeholders: teachers, students, and parents.

- To what extent is the written curriculum implemented in each classroom?
- Are state standards defined well enough to guide daily classroom instruction?
- Is local curriculum intentionally and effectively aligned with CCSS or state standards?
- Does it represent or identify highest-priority learning standards?
- Have those standards been sufficiently deconstructed into the classroom-level targets that students must achieve to obtain mastery of those standards? (See Activity 2.2 for practice in this area.)
- Is the curriculum balanced among the four different types of learning targets (knowledge, reasoning, skill, product), resulting in the use of a variety of assessment methods? Are teachers provided the resources and time needed to collaboratively work at refining the standards for classroom instruction?

It is also important to ensure that the curriculum is available to parents and students in versions written specifically for them. Although parents still want a comparison for how their child is doing against classmates, more parents are getting used to viewing student learning vis-á-vis attainment of standards. To support this view, curriculum documents translated to everyday language and in a user-friendly format can be posted on the refrigerator at home, and help parents not only know what their children are learning but also support them in that effort. Leaders can act in this area when they support teachers in curriculum mapping or grade-level/subject-area articulation activities to further clarify what is taught and assessed and when they provide structured time for teachers to work together to develop lessons geared toward the standards and aligned assessments.

In addition, as discussed in Action 2 in Part 2, it is important for leaders to ensure that all teachers are masters of the content knowledge they are assigned to teach. This need goes beyond being a foundation for good instruction; researchers have found that a foundation for the development of good classrooms assessments is also deep content knowledge (Ruiz-Primo, Furtak, Yin, Ayala, & Shavelson, 2010). Effective leaders arrange for subject-area professional development where needed and institute hiring practices that place a high priority on selecting candidates with strong backgrounds in curricular content as well as pedagogical knowledge and skill. (See Activity 3.3, "Verifying Teachers' Content Knowledge and Assessment Competence.")

Other ways leaders can act include the following:

- Verify that content standards drive classroom instruction (vs. a syllabus made up of chapter titles from a textbook) and that daily lessons deliver the scaffolding students need to attain mastery of those standards.
- Whenever not done so already, break down group achievement data into standard-by-standard information so schools can report individual student progress based on those same content standards.
- Ensure instruction is aimed at all targets in the written curriculum, not just those covered by the adopted texts or the standards assessed by the state for accountability purposes.

ACTIVITY 3.2

Implementing the Written Curriculum

PURPOSE

When the written curriculum is uniformly implemented the probability that the learning expectations for students are consistent across schools and classrooms increases. Without it we risk reverting to a teacher or classroom-driven curriculum. We believe that ensuring implementation and continued use of district-adopted curricula in every classroom of the school district is a responsibility best shared. The roles-based plan outlined here defines responsibilities for each member of your school's or district's education team. This activity provides ideas on how different roles/positions in the organization can help make the written curriculum of the state, district, or school become what is used to plan and deliver instruction.

TIME

Variable

MATERIALS NEEDED

Information or documents detailing the level of curriculum implementation in your school/district

SUGGESTED ROOM SETUP

Tables and chairs for easy discussion among members of the curriculum committee

DIRECTIONS

1. Gather information on the level of curriculum implementation in your school or district. There may be uniformity in certain schools and not others, in certain grade levels and departments and not others, or implementation issues may exist systemwide.

2. We suggest that you use these lists of responsibilities as the basis for self-study—to see if all roles are being fulfilled. If they are not, determine what needs to be done and by whom to guarantee quality implementation in every school. You can do this by discussing with your team to what extent each function has been carried by the specific role/job title.

Curriculum Office	Building Principal
• Make use of whatever tools and resources are provided by the state or other agencies to help disseminate and understand the standards. • Tap into state or CCSS professional development opportunities. • Whatever the written curriculum is or its source make it readily available in multiple ways and easily read for all subjects, all grade levels, K–12. • Provide ongoing training for teachers in understanding and teaching all learning targets. • Provide targeted training for teachers new to the district. • Provide "at a glance" sheets to teachers and within public documents such as parent handbooks to use with parents during back-to-school nights, conferences, etc. • Provide skill continuum documents over grade-level spans when appropriate. • Provide evidence the new curriculum improves student learning. • Provide sample classroom assessments and tasks linked to the written curriculum. • Carefully review all instructional materials for clear alignment and support of the written curriculum. • Ensure alignment of locally developed curriculum with state standards. • Link report card phrases to the written curriculum to ensure standards-based reporting. • Identify that content in texts and supplemental materials that does and does not align with and support standards and grade-level curriculum.	• Focus supervision and evaluation of classroom teaching on use of the curriculum in planning and delivering instruction and in assessing student progress. • Frequently observe and verify the use of the curriculum in instruction in the classroom. • Use the written curriculum as the foundation for intervention and student assistance programs. • Provide teachers common planning time to work together to plan lessons leading to the accomplishment of the standards. • Act as conduit between Curriculum Office and school staff. • Promote use of the written curriculum through personal knowledge of the specific objectives. • Help connect and align adopted curriculum with classroom practice through staff development, faculty meetings, vertical teaming groups, etc. • Help secure resources for teachers to help understand/teach the curriculum, as needed. • Call on curriculum specialists or master teachers to assist as necessary. • Encourage teachers to follow a process to "audit" classroom curriculum against the CCSS/state/adopted curriculum, if necessary. • Help ensure instructional materials support the written curriculum.
Classroom Teacher	**School Board Policies**
• Plan with, teach and assess using the written curriculum. • Use district documents as the basis for daily planning and formative and summative assessment. • Communicate the learning expectations to students and parents, regularly and in student and parent-friendly language. • Possess detailed knowledge of subject-area objectives and be able to classify the type of learning target. • Monitor each student's progress toward the content standards. • In summary, know it, teach it, and assess it.	• Develop curriculum implementation policy. • Align district policies/curriculum to state goals. • Ensure professional development policies support subject-specific training.

In addition, the following functions have roles to play in implementing the written curriculum:

Staff Development	Teacher Evaluation
• Clearly focus on curriculum implementation through a common training model for schools to follow. • In instructional strategies training (in math, science, reading, etc.), use standards as context/examples. • Offer professional development in content areas, linked to standards/curriculum. • Continue teacher involvement in curriculum revision/improvement, including deconstruction of standards. • Provide school-based training on units of study based on the curriculum. • Develop enrichment units/lessons and distribute them. • Continue training related to specific curricula. • Offer teachers an audit of building/classroom materials to ensure curriculum alignment.	• Continue to encourage staff to write professional growth goals related to curriculum implementation for formative evaluation. • Ensure summative evaluation criteria/indicators relate to planning lessons, teaching, and assessing the written curriculum. • Pre-/postconferences always focus in part on the intended learning, as drawn from the written curriculum.

 Available for download at **http://www.resources.corwin.com/ChappuisBalancedAssessment**

INDIVIDUAL LEADERSHIP ACTION 3:
Promote and communicate standards of quality for student assessments, helping teachers learn to assess accurately, and work to ensure that these standards are met in all school/district assessments. This includes ensuring the assessment literacy of teacher teams developing assessments for use across grade levels or subject areas.

It's not uncommon for a student or a parent to complain about the items or tasks on a teacher's test, citing them as unfair, off-target, or confusing. We've already stated that we believe that part of the teacher's professional competence should include knowing how to apply standards of quality to classroom assessment development or selection that would in effect minimize complaints about the quality of an assessment.

But, and this is the worst case scenario, the assessment job of classroom teachers can be unintentionally removed from their hands. In lieu of helping teachers become assessment literate, districts may substitute ready-made assessments narrowly designed to prepare for state tests or to generate additional summative, assessment *of* learning data. But quality classroom assessment is not about teachers administering more mini-versions of the state test or relying on common or interim or assessments as the only source of formative information.

So, it is important that part of the school leader's knowledge base is to be able to judge whether a given assessment adheres to quality standards. Regardless of the fact that most teachers have not been provided adequate training in classroom assessment, they still develop the great majority of their own assessments. Furthermore, selecting ready-made assessments these days is easier than simply picking questions from the back of the textbook or from other supplementary material. Websites offer test items and tasks to teachers in many subjects and grade levels, test item banks remain popular purchases for individual and group teacher test construction, and extending that, schools and districts build their own banks, pooling items from across the district. Who is minding the quality store when so much assessment content is available? Unless each teacher is able to evaluate items and assessments for quality, the door is left open for potential mismeasurement.

School leaders can evaluate any assessment developed or selected by teachers according to the five keys to quality classroom assessment discussed previously. (See Figure 1.1 in Part 1.)

ACTIVITY 3.3

Verifying Teachers' Content Knowledge and Assessment Competence

PURPOSE

This activity asks participants to answer three questions:

1. What questions could be asked in an interview with prospective teachers that would help school leaders evaluate their academic preparation to teach and assess the assigned subject(s)?

2. What questions can school leaders ask, or what evidence they should seek, to verify current teachers' mastery of the standards they are expected to teach and their level of assessment literacy in measuring those standards?

3. How can leaders assist teachers who are not currently masters of the standards or competent assessors?

TIME

1 hour

MATERIALS NEEDED

- Interview forms and teacher evaluation models/forms currently in use in your district
- Your district's comprehensive assessment plan, if available

SUGGESTED ROOM SETUP

- Tables and chairs set up for ease of discussion among participants
- Interactive whiteboards or flip charts and easels for capturing discussion points

DIRECTIONS

Think about and discuss the following questions:

- What should you reasonably expect the interview component of the overall hiring process to produce regarding useful information about the candidate's subject-matter knowledge?

- Given that, what questions could you design that would help inform you about the applicant's subject-matter knowledge? What is the range of acceptable answers to those questions?
- What should you reasonably expect the interview component to produce regarding useful information about the candidate's assessment competence?
- What questions could you design that would inform you about the applicant's assessment competence? What answers would you consider acceptable for that set of questions?
- Do you currently have a process for determining the subject knowledge and assessment competence of the teachers who already teach in your school or district?
- Is this process adequate?
- Does it need improving? If so, what questions do you need to ask? What evidence do you need to seek?
- What staff development and support do you provide for teachers who are not yet masters of the content standards or experienced assessors of the standards? Is it adequate? What improvements need to be made? Can you assign them to a position where they do have the content knowledge their students must master? Can you provide teachers with collaborative learning environments to become assessment literate?

CLOSURE

Whatever questions you might ask about subject-matter knowledge and assessment competence, consider the following points:

- Is there a link between what questions are asked in an employment interview and subsequent teacher evaluation? If not, should there be? Why or why not?
- Is there a link between those same questions, which in part act as expectations of teacher skills and knowledge, and the staff development program of your school or district? If not, should there be? Why or why not?

Look at the questions on some of the interview forms currently in use in your school or district to see if they include questions related to assessment. If they do, are the questions related to assessment *of* learning, assessment *for* learning, or both? If your district has a comprehensive assessment plan, check it to see if it spells out classroom assessment competencies. Also, consider asking teachers whom you believe already understand the principles of quality assessment to tell you what questions they think should be included in the interview.

 Available for download at **http://www.resources.corwin.com/ChappuisBalancedAssessment**

INDIVIDUAL LEADERSHIP ACTION 4:
Deepen your knowledge of formative assessment practices that involve students and work with staff to integrate them into daily instruction.

Over the years educators have been encouraged to think about assessment and instruction as hand in glove, to think about teaching as one seamless act melding curriculum, instruction, and assessment. In Part 2, we described seven strategies of assessment *for* learning (J. Chappuis, 2015). Beyond being grounded in the research that supports formative assessment, these strategies are also our best answer to teachers' frequently asked question, "Exactly how do I integrate assessment with instruction and truly make one an extension of the other?" The application of the seven strategies achieves just that in the classroom, with assessment becoming another form of good teaching.

Sometimes we see teachers using assessment *for* learning practices during learning, even though they have never been formally introduced to them. This presents an opportunity to help the teacher understand why that practice works or is supported in research, if he or she is unfamiliar with either. It also can be a good time to open the discussion wider about what else a teacher might do that is similar in effects on students. Here are some examples of what assessment-literate teachers do when applying the seven strategies of assessment *for* learning:

- Teachers understand and can articulate *in advance of teaching* the achievement targets students are to hit.
- *Students are informed regularly* about those targets in terms they can understand, in part through the study of the criteria by which their work will be evaluated, and samples of high-quality work. As a result, *students can describe what targets they are to hit* and what comes next in their learning.
- Both teacher and students use classroom assessment information to *revise and guide* teaching and learning.
- Teachers teach students the skills of self-assessment.
- Teachers provide students with descriptive feedback linked directly to the intended learning targets, giving them insight about current strengths and how to do better next time rather than giving evaluative feedback consisting only of marks and letter grades. Students have an opportunity to practice, using this feedback, before a summative assessment.
- Keep students connected to a vision of quality as the learning unfolds, continually defining for students what the learning expectations are for the lesson/unit.
- Involve students in their own assessment in ways that require them to think about their own progress, communicate their own understanding of what they have learned, and set goals to close the gap between where they are now relative to the intended learning and where they need to be to meet standards.
- Assessment-literate teachers teach students how to present their work/progress in conferences, have students create practice test items, and evaluate anonymous classroom work for quality—all examples of students being involved in assessment.
- Have students communicate the status of their own learning to interested adults through written journals, student-involved parent conferences, and portfolios that focus on growth toward the standards.

In the above list you may notice three characteristics of these and other formative practices:

1. Teachers can adjust their instruction quickly, while the learning is still going on, because the results of assessment *for* learning activities are often immediate.

2. The students who benefit from the adjustments are the same ones who were assessed, not a group in a later semester.

3. The students can also act on the results themselves to improve their own learning, particularly if they are given dedicated time to do so (S. Chappuis & Chappuis, 2008).

ACTIVITY 3.4

Communicating Learning Targets in Student-Friendly Language

PURPOSE

This activity is designed for use with a group of teachers to introduce and practice the process of converting a reasoning learning target into student-friendly language.

TIME

45–60 minutes (Can be broken into two parts, with the second part beginning at Step 5.)

MATERIALS NEEDED

The handout "Converting Learning Targets to Student-Friendly Language" (Figure 3.1); participants can also bring their content standards for one subject or class

SUGGESTED ROOM SETUP

Tables and chairs arranged so that teachers can work in job-alike groups

CONTEXT

The process of making learning targets clear to students can take many forms, which are explained fully in Chapter 2 of *Seven Strategies of Assessment* for *Learning* (J. Chappuis, 2015). This activity is useful when you want teachers to understand one way to help students answer the assessment *for* learning question, "Where am I going?" by defining key terms in a content standard or learning target.

CAUTION

The process is not a one-size-fits-all remedy for making targets clear to students. It is especially suited to the patterns of reasoning represented in each subject's content standards. More complex learning targets may require a rubric to fully define them as well as a process for converting the rubric into student-friendly language, which can be accomplished as a part of a learning team's work as they study one of the assessment texts explaining this (Arter & Chappuis, 2006, Chapter 3; J. Chappuis, 2015, Chapter 2; J. Chappuis et al., 2012, Chapter 7).

DIRECTIONS

1. Briefly describe the rationale for making learning targets clear to students. Explain that this activity shows one way to do that and that it is especially suited to learning targets that require students to reason. (See Figure 3.1.)

2. Distribute the handout (Figure 3.2) and explain the process, showing how it would work for the learning target "Summarize text."

3. Then ask teachers to select either "Infer" or "Hypothesize" and, working with a partner, to define the word and then translate it into language that their students would understand (Figure 3.3).

4. Ask volunteers to share both their definition and the student-friendly language. After hearing several examples, ask table groups to select one and come to consensus on both the definition and student-friendly language for it. Have tables share the consensus language.

5. Ask teachers to work with their subject-area colleagues (at the elementary level, ask teachers to select a subject area by grade level) to identify a content standard from their own curriculum that would benefit from this process. Have them use the process to create a definition of words needing defining and then to write the learning target in student-friendly language.

6. Ask volunteers to share the original learning target and their student-friendly version.

7. As closure you may wish to ask teachers to use the student-friendly versions they have created with students and come back together after a short time to discuss what they did with the targets and what they noticed happening with students as a result.

Figure 3.1   Converting Learning Targets to Student-Friendly Language

Select a learning target that would be made clearer by this process. Reasoning learning targets are often good candidates. Then use the following process to convert it into student-friendly language.

The Process

1. Identify the word(s) and/or phrase(s) needing clarification. Which terms will students struggle with? Imagine stating the target in its original form to your class. Then envision the degree of understanding reflected on faces throughout the room. At which word did they lose meaning?

2. Define the term(s) you have identified. Use a dictionary, your textbook, your state content standards document, or other reference materials specific to your subject. If you are working with a colleague, come to agreement on definitions.

3. Convert the definition(s) into language your students are likely to understand.

4. Turn the student-friendly definition into an "I" or a "We" statement: "I can _____"; "I am learning to _____"; or "We are learning to _____." Run it by a colleague for feedback.

5. Try the definition out with students. Note their responses. Refine as needed.

6. Let students have a go at this procedure occasionally, using learning targets you think they could successfully define and paraphrase. Make sure the definition they concoct is congruent with your vision of the target.

Source: Chappuis, Jan, *Seven Strategies of Assessment for Learning,* 1st Ed., © 2010, pp. 7, 22–24. Reprinted by permission of Pearson Education, Inc., New York, New York.

Figure 3.2   The Process in Action

Learning target: Summarize text.

Word to be defined: *Summarize*

Definition: To give a brief statement of the main ideas and significant details

Student-friendly language: I can summarize text. This means I can make a short statement of the main ideas and most important details from a passage I have read.

Learning target: Make predictions.

Word to be defined: *Prediction*

Definition: A statement saying that something will happen in the future

Student-friendly language: I can make predictions. This means I can use information from what I read to guess at what will happen next. (Or to guess what the author will tell me next.)

Source: Chappuis, Jan, *Seven Strategies of Assessment* for *Learning,* 1st Ed., © 2010, pp. 7, 22–24. Reprinted by permission of Pearson Education, Inc., New York, New York.

Figure 3.3   Your Turn

Working with a partner, select either *infer* or *hypothesize* and follow the process to convert it to student-friendly language.

Word to be defined: *Infer*

Definition:

Student-friendly language: I can infer. This means I can

Word to be defined: *Hypothesize*

Definition:

Student-friendly language: I can hypothesize. This means I can

---

Source: Chappuis, Jan, *Seven Strategies of Assessment* for *Learning,* 1st Ed., © 2010, pp. 7, 22–24. Reprinted by permission of Pearson Education, Inc., New York, New York.

 Available for download at **http://www.resources.corwin.com/ChappuisBalancedAssessment**

INDIVIDUAL LEADERSHIP ACTION 5:
Create the conditions necessary for the appropriate use and reporting of student achievement information, including report card grades.

Test scores and traditional report card grades do not communicate sufficient detail about student learning to support next steps in learning. But there are communication options available that can offer that support, including standards-based grading practices and using students as communicators of their own progress toward standards.

As a review, communication or feedback to students about their own progress falls into two broad categories: evaluative or descriptive. Finished student work, after the learning, receives a score or grade indicating its quality. This score or grade is considered *evaluative feedback*. During learning students need information focusing on current mastery, what needs work, and how to succeed at hitting the target. This information is *descriptive feedback*. With good descriptive feedback, teachers and parents also know students' strengths and areas for improvement and can use this information to guide them.

In the end, both evaluative and descriptive feedback are forms of communication, and both must be done accurately and effectively to be useful to their users. Leaders can help teachers understand both types of feedback and learn how to use both well in the classroom. But there are other communication challenges for leaders, too.

Grading and Reporting

If grades are to reflect something meaningful and serve a useful communications function, they must be based on accurate assessments. But grading practices themselves can present many difficult and potentially contentious issues. Unless resolved, these issues can result in inaccurate communication about student learning. The most common grading problems that lead to faulty grades are summarized in O'Connor's (2007) *A Repair Kit for Grading*.

When the report card grade obscures more than it reveals about achievement, we need to act to create the conditions needed to bring clarity and accuracy to both grading and communication about achievement. For example, if the current grading software program that teachers use contains routines that act as barriers to sound grading and reporting practices, then the obvious leadership challenge is to reprogram it or replace it. And it doesn't take a software program to provide the appearance of grades that are fair and precise; without a school or district policy on grading itself based on sound grading practices, various grading schemes can be at work, further confusing both students and parents about how good is good enough.

Schools and districts that have moved or are moving to new reporting systems based on student attainment of content standards can take steps to ensure both students and parents understand how student progress will now be reported. By comparing and contrasting for parents a traditional report card based on A–F letter grades with a new standards-based model, and describing the characteristics of and the philosophical foundation for each type of system, parents can better see the transition from one to the other. Informing students and parents of what is and is not factored into the report card grade also is important in building a common understanding. It helps to use as few coded messages as possible (B–, 79%, satisfactory, emerging, check+, etc.) and to always provide clear definitions of what those symbols mean when they are used.

ACTIVITY 3.5

A Rubric for Sound Grading Practice

PURPOSE

The rubric that follows supports the three principles for grading we recommend:

1. The purpose of grades is to communicate

2. Grades should communicate only about student achievement

3. Grades should reflect the current level of achievement

The rubric reflects what we support in sound grading practice—that is, grading practices that best communicate classroom assessment both *of* and *for* learning results. Any mark or grade is only as good as the assessment(s) on which it was based. For that reason, to use the rubric fully, it helps for both leaders and teachers to have a foundational knowledge of sound classroom assessment practices.

TIME

1 hour

MATERIALS NEEDED

- Copies of the grading rubric for each participant
- Copies of school/district grading policies

SUGGESTED ROOM SETUP

Tables and chairs set up for easy analysis and discussion among participants

DIRECTIONS

Use the rubric (Figure 3.4) as a discussion starter for both practice and policy. Analyze your staff practices to see how nearly they approach the stated grading guidelines. Analyze your current school/district policies on grading regarding what is currently in them relative to the rubric and what is missing. What steps would you need to take to align your grading policies and staff practices with these guidelines?

Figure 3.4   Rubric for Sound Grading Practice

Criterion	Beginning	Development	Fluent
1. Organizing the Gradebook	The evidence of learning (e.g., a gradebook) is entirely organized by sources of information (tests, quizzes, homework, labs, etc.).	The evidence of learning (e.g., a gradebook) is organized by sources of information mixed with specific content standards.	The evidence of learning (e.g., a gradebook) is completely organized by student learning outcomes (content standards, benchmarks, grade level indicators, curriculum expectations).
2. Including Factors in the Grade	Overall summary grades are based on a mix of achievement and nonachievement factors (e.g., timeliness of work, attitude, effort, cheating). Nonachievement factors have a major impact on grades.	Overall summary grades are based on a mix of achievement and nonachievement factors, but achievement counts a lot more.	Overall summary grades are based on achievement only.
	Extra credit points are given for extra work completed; without connection to extra learning.	Some extra credit points are given for extra work completed; some extra credit work is used to provide extra evidence of student learning.	Extra credit work is evaluated for quality and is only used to provide extra evidence of learning. Credit is not awarded merely for completion of work.
	Cheating, late work, and missing work result in a zero (or lower score) in the gradebook. There is no opportunity to make up work, except in a few cases.	Cheating, late work, and missing work result in a zero (or lower score) in the gradebook. But there is an opportunity to make up work and replace the zero or raise the lower score.	Cheating, late work, and missing work is recorded as "incomplete" or "not enough information" rather than "0." There is an opportunity to replace an incomplete with a score without penalty.
	Borderline cases are handled by considering nonachievement factors.	Borderline cases are handled by considering a combination of nonachievement factors and collecting evidence of student learning.	Borderline grade cases are handled by collecting additional evidence of student achievement, not by counting nonachievement factors.
3. Considering Assessment Purpose	Everything each student does is given a score, and every score goes into the final grade. There is no distinction between scores on practice work (formative assessment or many types of homework) and scores on work to demonstrate level of achievement (summative assessment).	Some distinctions are made between formative (practice such as homework) and summative assessment, but practice work still constitutes a significant part of the grade.	Student work is assessed frequently (formative assessment) and graded occasionally (summative assessment). Scores on formative assessments and other practice work (e.g., homework) are used descriptively to inform teachers and students of what has been learned and the next steps in learning. Grades are based only on summative assessments.

Criterion	Beginning	Development	Fluent
4. Considering Most Recent Information	All assessment data is cumulative and used in calculating a final summative grade. No consideration is given to identifying or using the most current information.	More current evidence is given consideration at times but does not entirely replace out-of-date evidence.	Most recent evidence completely replaces out-of-date evidence when it is reasonable to do so. For example, how well students write at the end of the grading period is more important than how well they wrote at the beginning, and later evidence of improved content understanding is more important than early evidence.
5. Summarizing Information and Determining Final Grade	The gradebook has a mixture of ABC, percentages, +/−, and/or rubric scores with no explanation of how they are to be combined into a final summary grade.	The gradebook may or may not have a mixture of symbols, but there is some attempt, even if incomplete, to explain how to combine them.	The gradebook may or may not have a mix of symbol types, but there is a sound explanation of how to combine them.
	Rubric scores are converted to percentages when averaged with other scores, or there is no provision for combining rubric and percentage scores.	Rubric scores are not directly converted to percentages; some type of decision rule is used, the final grade many times does not best depict level of student achievement.	Rubric scores are converted to a final grade using a decision rule that results in an accurate depiction of the level of student attainment of the learning targets.
	Final summary grades are based on a curve—a student's place in the rank order of student achievement.	Final grades are criterion referenced, not norm referenced. They are based on preset standards such as A = 90%–100% and B = 80%–89%. But, there is no indication of the necessity to ensure shared meaning of symbols—i.e., there is no definition of each standard.	Final grades are criterion referenced, not norm referenced. They are based on preset standards with clear descriptions of what each symbol means. These descriptions go beyond A = 90%–100% and B = 80%–89%; they describe what A, B, and so on performance looks like.
	Final grades for special needs students are not based on learning targets as specified in the individual education program (IEP).	There is an attempt to base final grades for special needs students on learning targets in the IEP, but the attempt is not always successful, or it is not clear to all parties that modified learning targets are used to assign a grade.	Final grades for special needs students are criterion referenced, and indicate level of attainment of the learning goals as specified in the IEP. The targets on which grades are based are clear to all parties.
	Final summary grades are based on calculation of mean (average) only.	The teacher understands various measures of central tendency, but may not always choose the best one to accurately describe student achievement.	The teacher understands various measures of central tendency (average, median, mode) and understands when each is the most appropriate one to use to accurately describe student learning.

(Continued)

Figure 3.4   (Continued)

Criterion	Beginning	Development	Fluent
6. Verifying Assessment Quality	There is little evidence of consideration of the accuracy/quality of the individual assessments on which grades are based.	The teacher tries to base grades on accurate assessment results only but may not consciously understand all the features of a sound assessment.	Grades are based only on accurate assessment results. Questionable results are not included.
	Quality standards for classroom assessment are not considered and the teacher has trouble articulating standards for quality.	Some standards of quality are adhered to in judging the accuracy of the assessment results on which grades are based. The teacher can articulate some of these standards, or uses standards for quality assessment intuitively, but has trouble articulating why an assessment is sound.	The teacher can articulate standards of quality and can show evidence of consideration of these standards in his or her classroom assessments: • clear and appropriate learning targets • clear and appropriate for users and uses • sound assessment design (proper method, quality exercises, sound sampling, minimum bias) • effective communication of results
	Assessments are rarely modified for special needs students when such modifications would provide much more accurate information about student learning.	Assessments are modified for special needs students, but the procedures used may not result in accurate information and/or match provisions in the IEP.	Assessments are modified for special needs students in ways that match instructional modifications described in IEPs. Such modifications result in generating accurate information on student achievement.
7. Student Involvement	Grades are a surprise to students because (a) students don't understand the bases on which grades are determined; (b) students have not been involved in their own assessment (learning targets are not clear to them, and/or they do not self-assess and track progress toward the targets); or (c) teacher feedback is only evaluative (a judgment of level of quality) and includes no descriptive component.	Grades are somewhat of a surprise to students because student-involvement practices and descriptive feedback are too limited to give them insights into the nature of the learning targets being pursued and their own performance.	Grades are not a surprise to students because (a) students understand the basis for the grades received; (b) students have been involved in their own assessment throughout the process (they understand the learning targets they are to hit, self-assess in relation to the targets, track their own progress toward the targets, and/or talk about their progress); and/or (c) teacher communication to students is frequent, descriptive, and focuses on what they have learned as well as the next steps in learning. Descriptive feedback is related directly to specific and clear learning targets.

Source: Based on suggestions from Ken O'Connor (personal communication, 2003).

ACTIVITY 3.6

When Grades Don't Match the State Assessment Results

PURPOSE

Often we see students with low report card grades but high standardized test scores and vice versa. This activity has participants explore reasons why there might be a disconnect between report card grades and state test scores.

TIME

10–20 minutes

MATERIALS NEEDED

If available, information showing the relationship/disparity between report card grades and state test results

SUGGESTED ROOM SETUP

Tables and chairs for ease of discussion/participation

DIRECTIONS

Together with your teachers read the scenario and then discuss the following questions.

Scenario: Students consistently get high grades but fail to meet competency on a state test. Or the reverse, students get low grades but demonstrate a high level of competency on the state test.

- Why might the situation be occurring? Consider the extent to which conditions for sound communication are violated.
- Are other standards of quality assessment being violated?

Possible reasons: (1) The state assessment only includes achievement, while grades might include factors other than achievement, such as absences. (2) Class instruction and assessment may include more or different content than the standards measured in the state assessment, meaning classroom assessments might measure different targets than the state assessment. (3) The classroom assessments underpinning the grades aren't accurate. (4) It is unclear how the state performance standard cutoff relates to teachers' grading cutoffs. (5) They were given at different times and might not match with respect to the content students have encountered in the school/instructional calendar.

CLOSURE

Discuss what you can do in your school or district to deal with this situation.

Possible solutions: (1) Clarify state assessment and classroom learning targets. Do they match? If not, should they? Is instruction aligned? (2) Check classroom assessments for accuracy—do they meet the five keys to quality classroom assessment? (3) Calibrate classroom assessments to the state assessment so that teachers and students know the level needed to perform on classroom assessments to meet state standards.

 Available for download at **http://www.resources.corwin.com/ChappuisBalancedAssessment**

INDIVIDUAL LEADERSHIP ACTION 6:
Form or participate in peer learning groups to practice observing and evaluating teacher classroom assessment competencies.

Evaluating teachers' classroom assessment competence is not yet a norm for many districts. Whether teacher evaluation is summative in nature, using a traditional observational checklists of criteria and indicators, or whether it is a formative model that relies on personal/professional growth goals as the structure for the evaluation, or a hybrid of the two, accountability for assessment competence, particularly at the classroom level, is often absent. Whatever supervision and evaluation model is in place, if something is worth knowing and doing properly in the classroom, especially something that can either harm or help students, solid guidance is called for. Specifically, principals need to know if teachers can do successfully the following:

1. Attend to the purpose of each assessment given, who will use the results, and in what way.

2. Address the learning targets being assessed and explain why they are important to assess.

3. Select proper assessment methods for the content and type of target.

4. Assure accuracy of the results with good design, proper sampling, and a minimum of bias.

5. Involve students in the assessment process.

6. Communicate assessment results to meet the needs of a variety of audiences.

7. Provide assessment criteria to students in terms they understand.

8. Provide descriptive feedback to students.

9. Use formative and summative data effectively to guide instruction and improve learning.

10. Use sound grading practices.

See Figure 2.15 as the foundation for this list. There are also two caveats to consider:

1. The elephant in the room as we have alluded to before is that most teachers haven't been given the opportunity to learn these things. So holding teachers accountable for things they haven't learned or been exposed to obviously is

something to avoid. If that is the case, a comprehensive plan of professional development to address the deficits as well a plan to re-tool the evaluation instruments is called for.

2. Furthermore, the models of adult learning we provide in schools today (in-service) are constricted by both time and resources and, as a result, take forms of professional development that often fail to transfer into classroom practice. It's a serious leadership challenge: a gap in the skill set of many teachers, coupled with a lack of time and/or resources for the needed professional development to fill the gap.

When evidence suggests that teachers do these things well a principal knows that quality assessment is a priority in the classroom and that the teacher understands the use of assessment *for* learning to improve student learning. When the principal holds regular discussions with teachers about these practices and is capable of providing supportive, meaningful feedback to staff, regardless of the teacher evaluation model in place, conversations in the school begin to center on the importance of using assessment in ways that contribute to learning, beyond final report card grades.

Expecting students to master standards requires teachers who are competent, confident masters of those standards. Whether hiring new teachers or verifying current teachers' mastery, leaders need to know how to do the verification (see Activity 3.3). If this process identifies teachers who are not masters of the standards they are to teach, leadership will need to provide a means for these teachers to become competent, confident masters of those standards.

Teaching applicants typically answer many questions, both in writing and in interviews. Questions related to classroom management, instructional skill, and issues of student discipline are common. Questions related to the candidate's mastery of content knowledge and development and use of quality assessments necessary for the specific teaching assignment are sometimes overlooked. Frequently, evidence of content mastery and assessment literacy is gathered from college transcripts, previous teaching assignments, or candidate portfolios to help inform the hiring decision.

ACTIVITY 3.7

Should Teachers Be Held Accountable for Assessment Competence Through Evaluation?

PURPOSE

The more frequent debate centers on whether student standardized test scores should be used as part of teacher evaluation. This leadership team activity asks you as school leaders to think about whether teachers should be evaluated for assessment competence and if so, what the criteria for that evaluation should include. Teacher evaluation criteria and instruments vary greatly and may or may not contain indicators of classroom assessment competence.

TIME

45–60 minutes

MATERIALS NEEDED

- Interactive whiteboard or flip chart
- Copies for each participant of the forms you use for teacher evaluation

SUGGESTED ROOM SETUP

Tables and chairs set for ease of discussion among participants

DIRECTIONS

Collect copies of the forms used for teacher evaluation in your school or district. Using the forms, make a separate list of the criteria that relate to assessment competence that are currently included.

In your group, discuss the following question:

Should teachers be held accountable for assessment competence through evaluation?

1. If your answer is "Yes," begin to list criteria, in addition to what may already be included, that you believe should be part of the evaluation document. The criteria would describe the specific knowledge and/or skills that you would want teachers to be able to demonstrate routinely in assessment. In Activity 2.3, you reviewed indicators of sound classroom assessment practice. These same indicators can be underpinnings for the criteria you establish in the evaluation document.

2. If your answer is "No," explain why you do not believe assessment competence should be part of teacher evaluation.

CLOSURE

This issue, and therefore the activity itself, may be complicated by the fact that many schools and districts no longer use a summative form or process for teacher evaluation. The traditional classroom observation by the principal and checklist with criteria/indicators used for pre- and/or postevaluation conferences about individual strengths and areas for improvement has been replaced in some schools. In many cases, evaluation systems rely more on formative processes, where the teacher selects a few, focused professional-growth goals or instructional goals, sometimes in partnership with the supervisor. Indicators of assessment competence would not necessarily be part of that model or others similar to it. If that is the case in your system, what other ways can schools and districts ensure each teacher is a competent assessor of student learning?

To assist those who wish to add assessment competence to their summative evaluation, the main question to be addressed is, "What are the indicators of competence we want to see demonstrated?" You can compare answers generated in this activity to indicators in several of the other activities in this guide, as well as to the list of principles of assessment *for* learning.

INDIVIDUAL LEADERSHIP ACTION 7:
Review and examine current school/district assessment-related policies for alignment to sound assessment practice, and encourage revision as needed.

Policy drives practice. If leaders want quality assessment practices in every classroom then district and school policies must support the implementation and continued use of such practices.

Many policies at both the school and the district level have the potential to either support or hinder the effective use of sound assessment practice. Further, policies can either support each other, acting in concert as a system of beliefs and practices, or they can act in opposition to each other, creating inconsistency and even conflict. It is part of the school leader's assessment responsibilities to revise policies so they provide a framework for sound practice and act in unison with each other. In fact, without policy support, assessment reform initiatives may flounder. Leaders are more likely to succeed at this task if they approach it with three perspectives in mind:

1. How leaders view the role of the policy manual is pivotal. School and district policy can be seen as far more than just the regulatory compliance arm of the organization. Beyond fulfilling the legal requirements of the state and federal governments, policy can serve as an implementation tool for strategic planning efforts and can be used as one of many strategies to help the vision become reality. It provides an opportunity to set and communicate standards, expectations, and the priorities most relevant to student achievement and can help educate the local community.

2. Assessment systems need to be planned as just that: systems with connected parts all working toward a common goal. District policy manuals and faculty handbooks should be approached from the same perspective. The elements all need to fit together, which requires thinking about policies beyond revising one at a time or revising each only in response to some district crisis or legislative enactment.

3. A written comprehensive assessment plan clarifies the purpose of assessment and how it fits into effective teaching and learning. Essential for assessment reform is a document that states assessment beliefs and provides guiding principles and policies for both large-scale testing and classroom practice based on that set of beliefs.

Policies that have a strong connection with student assessment and that can be reviewed for appropriateness and congruence include the following:

- Curriculum development
- Curriculum adoption
- Assessment
- Grading
- Professional development
- Hiring
- Teacher evaluation
- Student placement
- Communicating student progress
- Program evaluation
- IEP
- Strategic planning

- Pupil records
- Attendance
- Grouping for instruction
- Gifted/talented
- Lesson planning
- Promotion and retention
- Parent involvement

- Student selection
- Remediation and intervention
- Accountability
- Instruction
- Graduation requirements
- Homework
- Instructional materials

ACTIVITY 3.8

Using School/District Policies to Support Quality Assessment

PURPOSE

This activity requests that your team review a series of school/district policies, which all have a connection in some way to assessment. Some are more complete than others; some are more current and better written than others. All are examples of policies at the district level, although school-level administrators can also make use of this activity simply by shifting the emphasis to school-level policies contained in a faculty handbook. By reviewing the policies with an eye toward how they could be rewritten or improved to be more supportive of quality assessment, your team practices building the framework to help support quality assessment.

One of the objectives of this activity and in working with policy in general is to see policies as a systemic whole, where the elements (in this case the policies themselves) hang together, all working toward a common purpose. Not approaching the policy manual in that way risks having policies in opposition to each other: An attendance policy may contradict a grading policy, or a promotion/retention policy may conflict with a policy on student assessment that is grounded in a specific set of belief statements.

Last, the district-level policies in this activity are just that; some context is missing without the implementation procedures that usually accompany policies and provide the specifics of how the policy is to be applied. However, the underlying concepts and ideas are apparent in each example. The intention of the activity is not to perfect each policy but, rather, to get some practice in reviewing policies with quality assessment as the filter.

TIME

90 minutes

MATERIALS NEEDED

Optional: policies from your school or district

SUGGESTED ROOM SETUP

Tables and chairs

DIRECTIONS

Before starting this activity, it will be helpful for your team to list a set of criteria to use when reviewing these policies (and any other policies you may choose to use from your local school or district). What is the group looking to achieve in assessment through school or district policies? What would constitute a strong policy? For example, your team might generate policy review criteria in the form of questions. The list that follows is a start, but other considerations may be important to your team.

Does this policy

- support the vision of assessment in the school or district?
- have a direct impact on student learning?
- have an impact on or connection to other policies that need to be considered?
- encourage the use of multiple measures of student learning, creating judgments made about students with combinations of data sources?
- require clear, meaningful, and frequent communication about learning?
- link standards, instruction, and assessment?
- require any specialized professional development?

Figure 3.5 shows the same set of criteria in the graphic organizer that may be useful. Recognize that each of these criteria or those your team may generate might not be relevant or apply to each policy under review. After finalizing your list of criteria, read the first policy in this activity. Then pause and consider the following three questions with your team. Do this with the remainder of the sample policies in this activity. Use the criteria developed by your team to help answer the questions for each policy review.

1. What are the strong points of the policy the way it is currently written?

2. What are the weak areas of the policy?

3. What language could be omitted, and what language might be added to make it more supportive of sound assessment?

Policy 2101—Student Retention/Promotion

As the ability to read proficiently is the basic foundation for success in school, as it is indeed throughout life, it is the goal of the primary school, the first three (3) grades, to teach each child to read independently with understanding by the time he or she finishes the third grade. It is within this period when retention of a youngster in a grade can be most valuable. Teachers, taking into account factors such as achievement, mental age, chronological age, emotional wellness, and social and physical maturity may find it advisable in the case of some students to retain a child once or twice during this period. By following this policy, the district will find some children completing the first three grades in 4 years and some in 5 as well as the majority who will finish in the regular 3-year period.

With the preceding as a basic policy, retention after the third grade should only be a problem in those cases where a student is not achieving and meeting the grade standards of which he or she is capable. In cases where it is contemplated holding a student in the same grade for an extra year, the teacher should notify the parents as early in the year as possible but not later than the end of the third quarter.

Figure 3.5   Policy Review Organizer

Name and Number of Policy _____		
Does this policy . . .	**Yes/No**	**Comments**
1. Support the vision of assessment in the school or district?		
2. Have a direct impact on student learning?		
3. Have an impact on or connection to other policies that need to be considered?		
4. Encourage the use of multiple measures of student learning, creating judgments made about students with combinations of data sources?		
5. Require clear, meaningful, and frequent communication about learning?		
6. Link standards, instruction, and assessment?		
7. Require any specialized professional development?		
Any other questions?		

No student shall be retained for more than 2 years in the same grade.

Since it is the responsibility of the school to adjust the work in each grade to the child's individual needs and ability to provide an equal educational opportunity for all children, no arbitrary policy of promotion is suggested. Promotion should be made for grade to grade, based on a consideration of the best interest of the student concerned.

The following factors shall be taken into consideration: achievement, mental age, chronological age, emotional wellness, and social and physical maturity. The curriculum should be so broad on each grade level that the needs of bright students are met, as well as the needs of average and slow students. Therefore, when accepting pupils who are new to district schools, the principal should make the best placement possible on the basis of the information he or she can obtain.

Policy 2102—Lesson Plans

To ensure proper planning and continuity of instruction, the board requires that each teacher prepare lesson plans for daily instruction. To facilitate more effective instruction, lesson plans must be prepared in advance of the actual class presentation. The format for the lesson plan will be specified by the building principal and shall be reviewed on a regular basis. The plan book must be readily available when a substitute teacher is needed.

Policy 2103—Class Rank

The board acknowledges the usefulness of a system of computing grade point averages and class ranking for secondary school graduates to inform students, parents, and others of their relative academic placement among their peers.

The board authorizes a system of class ranking, by grade point average, for student in Grades 9 through 12. Class rank shall be computed by the final grade except that nonnumerical marks/grades shall be excluded from the calculation of the grade point average.

A student's grade point average shall be reported on his or her term grade report. Such calculations may also be used for recognizing individual students for their achievement.

Policy 2104—Homework

The board believes that homework is a constructive tool in the teaching/learning process when geared to the age, health, abilities, and needs of students. Purposeful assignments not only enhance student achievement but also develop self-discipline and associated good working habits. As an extension of the classroom, homework must be planned and organized, must be viewed as purposeful to the students, and must be evaluated and returned to the student in a timely manner.

The purposes of homework assignments, the basis for evaluating the work performed and the guidelines and/or rules should be made clear to the student at the time of the assignment.

The school principal shall establish guidelines that clarify the nature and use of homework assignments to improve school achievement.

Makeup work, due to illness, is not to be considered as homework. Students shall be given the opportunity to make up assignments missed during excused absences.

Policy 2106—Grading and Progress Reports

The board believes that the cooperation of school and home is a vital ingredient in the growth and education of the student and recognizes the responsibility to keep parents informed of student personal development/work habits, as well as academic progress in school.

The issuance of grades and progress reports on a regular basis serves as the basis for continuous evaluation of the student's performance and determining changes that should be made to effect improvement. These reports shall be designed to provide information that will be helpful to the student, teacher, counselor, and parent. For Grades 9 through 12, the district shall comply with the marking/grading system incorporated into the statewide standardized high school transcript. The superintendent may consider alternative grading/progress reports. A student's grade point shall be reported for each term, individually and cumulatively.

The board directs the superintendent to establish a system of reporting student progress and shall require all staff members to comply with such a system as a part of their teaching responsibility.

If classroom participation is used as the basis of mastery of an objective, a student's grades may be adversely affected by an absence, provided that on the day of the excused absence, there was a graded participation activity. If the teacher does not so advise students in writing, the teacher may not use attendance and participation in the grading process. Teachers shall consider circumstances pertaining to the student's inability to attend school. No student grade shall be reduced or credit denied for disciplinary reasons only rather than for academic reasons, unless due process of law is provided. Individual students, who feel that an unjust application of attendance or tardiness factors has been made, may follow the appeal process for resolving the differences. Academic appeals have no further step for appeal.

Policy 2107—Instruction

Effective Communication About Student Achievement

_____ School District is a standards-driven district with the goal of communicating effectively about student achievement. It is the intent of the district to provide timely, understandable, and meaningful information about student progress towards clearly articulated achievement standards to students, parents, educational professionals and third parties with interest. Grading and reporting practices represent one of a variety of ways to communicate student progress toward standards and may serve the following purpose(s):

- Communication of the achievement status of students to parents/guardians in ways that describe progress toward district standards and provide an accurate focus on learning
- Information students can use for self-evaluation and improvement

- Data for the selection, identification, or grouping of students for certain educational paths or programs
- Information for evaluation of the effectiveness of instructional programs

Grading and reporting provide important information about student progress, but there is no single best way of communicating about student achievement. The district will use a variety of ways to deliver information about student achievement to intended users. All information users are important and are entitled to timely and accurate achievement data: Some may require greater detail about achievement than can be provided by grades and test scores to make informed decisions. The following illustrate different types of communication about student achievement:

- Checklists of standards
- Narrative descriptions
- Portfolios of various kinds
- Report card grades
- Student conferences

All practices related to communication about student achievement should be carried out according to the best current understanding and application of the research. The district will provide staff members ongoing professional development needed to gain that understanding.

Grading and Reporting

The district's policy and procedures on communication about student achievement, specifically grading and reporting practices, are based on the principles that

- individual achievement of clearly stated learning targets should be the only basis for grades, providing an accurate reflection of what each student knows and can do; the effectiveness of the communication is determined by the accuracy of the information about student achievement.
- other characteristics (effort, behavior, attendance, attitude, etc.) should not be included in grades but should be reported separately.
- different users and decision makers of achievement data need information in different forms at different times to make their decisions.
- grading and reporting should always be done in reference to specified achievement targets, comparing students' performance against a standard rather than against other students in the class (on a curve).
- grades should be calculated to ensure that the grade each student receives is a fair reflection of what he or she knows and can do, emphasizing the most recent summative assessment information.
- consideration shall be given to the use of appropriate grade calculation procedures to ensure that assigned grades reflect the intended importance of each learning goal.
- grades have some value as incentives but no value as punishments.

During the first week of classes, teachers shall provide students and parents with a written syllabus of learning expectations and grading criteria in clear, easily understandable language, indicating how summative assessment throughout the grading period will be calculated into course grades. Teachers shall discuss classroom assessment practices with students, in an age appropriate manner, at the beginning of instruction.

The superintendent shall develop written procedures that support the district policy on Communicating Effectively about Student Achievement.

 Available for download at **http://www.resources.corwin.com/ChappuisBalancedAssessment**

THINKING ABOUT ASSESSMENT: SUPPORT RESOURCES FOR PART 3

The following resources relate directly to the content presented in Part 3. They are intended to either deepen understanding or assist leaders in implementing a balanced assessment system.

ACTIVITY 3.9

Auditing for Balance in Classroom Curriculum and Assessment

PURPOSE

Often when teachers are introduced to a new (or different) standards-aligned curriculum, they quickly identify one of the primary road block to implementation: "When am I going to find time to teach *all this*?" The following activity provides a process by which teachers can compare what they currently teach and assess to the content of a new or existing curriculum to determine the following:

- Where their instruction and assessment already align
- What parts of the curriculum they need to add
- Which instructional activities, targets and assessments they can eliminate
- What role current texts and supplementary materials play in daily instruction

Is there balance among the written curriculum targets and the assessment methods used to assess them? To complete the activity, teachers need to have created their current personal curriculum map for the year or course, including the content and skills they will teach and assessments they will use for each.

TIME

2–3 hours, depending on the scope of the comparison

MATERIALS NEEDED

- Each teacher's current curriculum plan, map, or syllabus for the year or course, including content and skills taught and assessments used
- Numbered list of the state/district curriculum standards/grade-level learning targets for each subject to be addressed

SUGGESTED ROOM SETUP

- Tables and chairs set for ease of discussion among participants
- Interactive whiteboards or easels with flip charts and markers to record discussion and decision making

DIRECTIONS

Data Gathering

1. *New and current curriculum—Where's the match?* Compare your curriculum map's list of content and skills to the numbered list of the new curriculum standards/grade-level learning targets. On your curriculum map, highlight those content and skill entries that show up on the list. Next, go back through the highlighted content and skill entries and write the number of the new curriculum standard(s)/grade-level learning target(s) next to each highlighted content and skill on your curriculum map to show the match.

2. *Instruction—How's the balance?* Working with the content and skill entries you highlighted on your curriculum map in Step 1, determine the amount of emphasis each new standard or grade-level learning target receives in your current teaching. Is it about right, given its relative importance to everything else students must learn and its emphasis in state and district assessments? Is it overrepresented? Underrepresented? Not present at all? Mark the corresponding column on the chart, "Comparing the Classroom Curriculum to District/State Standards."

3. *Assessment—How's the balance?* Again working with the content and skill entries you highlighted in Step 1, refer to the assessments students take over the course of the year. Is each new standard or grade-level learning target sufficiently sampled, given its relative importance to everything else students must learn and its emphasis in state and district assessments? Is it oversampled? Undersampled? Or not assessed at all? Mark the corresponding column on the chart, "Comparing the Classroom Curriculum to District/ State Standards."

Decision Making

4. *What to leave out?* Examine the content and skills you *didn't* highlight in Step 1 to determine which can and should be eliminated from your curriculum map. If you can address the new curriculum in less than the full year, consider which of these content and skills can and should remain in your teaching plan.

5. *What to adjust?* Use the information in Figure 3.6, "Comparing the Classroom Curriculum to District/State Standards" gathered in Steps 2 and 3, to rework your curriculum map.

Figure 3.6 Comparing the Classroom Curriculum to District/State Standards

Standard/ Grade-Level Learning Target	Instruction and Activities				Assessment			
	Right amount of emphasis	Too much emphasis	Not enough emphasis	Not present	Sufficient sample	Oversampled	Under-sampled	Not sampled
1.								
2.								
3.								
4.								
5.								
6.								
7.								

Available for download at **http://www.resources.corwin.com/ChappuisBalancedAssessment**

ACTIVITY 3.10

Assessment Leadership Success Indicators

PURPOSE

This activity helps leaders focus on the Individual Leadership Actions in assessment in light of current knowledge and experience. Working with this activity in teams may then extend to in collaborative learning and practice in commonly identified areas targeted for improvement.

TIME

15–30 minutes

MATERIALS NEEDED

Copies of the Assessment Leadership Success Indicators along with the self-reflection sheets

SUGGESTED ROOM SETUP

This activity can be done within a group attending a meeting, as part of an administrative in-service or the activity can be completed on your own time and the information passed on to the central office for later discussion or aggregation of results

DIRECTIONS

Read through the list of Assessment Leadership Success Indicators. They are aligned to the Seven Individual Leadership Actions for School Leaders. If anything is unclear, seek clarification from Part 3 readings or from your colleagues. Then consider the following questions:

1. Based on your current experience, what do you see as your areas of greatest strength on the list of indicators?

2. Given that, how can your experience and strengths contribute to the district/school achieving a balanced, quality assessment system?

3. What areas as defined in the indicators do you think need strengthening?

4. What support or resources do you need to do so?

5. How will the strengthening of these areas assist you as a leader in the district's or the school's establishment of a balanced assessment system?

Individual Leadership Action: Deepen Understanding of a Balanced Assessment System and the Conditions to Achieve It

The leader

- can articulate a model of a local assessment system that calls for balance, quality assessment, and student involvement.

- knows the differences among and the appropriate uses of classroom, common, interim/benchmark, and annual assessment, including the key decisions to be made, the decision makers, and the kinds of information needed to inform those decisions.

Individual Leadership Action: Promote Clear Achievement Standards and Their Use

The leader

- knows why clear achievement targets underpin a quality assessment system, can outline the attributes of quality standards, and knows how to ensure quality in local assessments.
- can communicate the roles of both summative and formative assessment in standards-based schools.
- values the transformation of learning targets into student- and family-friendly versions and can describe a process to transform them.

Individual Leadership Action: Promote and Communicate Standards for Assessment Quality in All Levels of Assessment and Promote Assessment Literacy Across All Classrooms

The leader

- describes the five keys to quality assessment, how they relate to one another, and why they should underpin assessments at all levels.
- asks questions about all school data sources to help determine if issues of quality were addressed.
- knows how to select or develop assessments that meet standards of assessment quality

Individual Leadership Action: Deepen Knowledge of Formative Assessment Practices That Involve Students

The leader

- can provide examples of what formative assessment *for* learning looks like in the classroom, including how students might be involved.

Individual Leadership Action: Create the Conditions Necessary for the Appropriate Use and Reporting of Student Achievement Information

The leader

- differentiates between evaluative and descriptive feedback and can explain why it is important to balance them in the classroom.
- understands the meaning of the various test scores and other forms of evidence of learning available to them and can interpret those scores correctly regarding the inferences about student achievement each permits.

- understands the differences between sound and unsound classroom grading practices.
- sees the connection between standards-based reporting processes and standards-based assessments and works to develop such a communication system.
- knows how to administer assessments in a manner that ensures all students an equal opportunity to demonstrate competence.
- understands the conditions for effective adult learning in schools that improves instruction and student learning.
- knows that professional development that works calls for a long-term *process* that teaches new ideas and strategies through hands-on practice, coaching, and collaboration.
- provides leadership support for professional development by ensuring sufficient resources (time and materials) for adult learning and promoting support for ongoing improvement.
- understands the meaning of the results of all tests used in the school and how to interpret them correctly.
- knows how to turn assessment results into useful information and how to link them directly to instructional decision making at classroom, interim/benchmark, and annual levels of assessment use.

Individual Leadership Action: Form or Participate in Peer Learning Groups to Practice Observing and Evaluating Teacher Classroom Assessment Competencies

The leader

- explains standards of sound classroom assessment practice that evaluations of teacher performance can or should be based on.
- develops interview questions that relate to the classroom assessment literacy of candidates for teaching positions. Knows what questions to ask about assessment quality and the effective use of assessment to promote learning and is prepared to interpret candidates' answers regarding their qualifications.
- creates ways to observe, analyze, evaluate, and provide feedback on classroom assessment process and artifacts (assessment instruments).

Individual Leadership Action: Review and Examine Current School/District Assessment-Related Policies for Alignment to Sound Assessment Practice, and Encourage Revision as Needed

The leader

- knows the policies that contribute to assessment balance and quality and effective use and is able to draft those statements for review, evaluation, and adoption.
- knows how to translate policies into procedures and guidelines that honor the intent of the policy.

 Available for download at **http://www.resources.corwin.com/ChappuisBalancedAssessment**

Action Planning for Assessment Balance and Quality

PURPOSE

Through the activities in this guide you have been reflecting on and discussing your current situation as well as your vision for the future, thinking about where you want your district or school to be relative to student assessment. You can transfer to a written action plan your team's analysis of your current system as well as your goals for a new system. The work to be completed for the new system will vary based on the profile you created and how far you have already progressed. Some leadership teams will be able to take action on their own; others may want to bring into the process a larger group of district or school stakeholders. Still others may first need to educate their peers or the instructional staff about the need for and promise of assessment balance and quality.

Like the district curriculum guide or set of state standards that can collect dust on top of the file cabinet in classroom where teachers define their own curriculum, there is no guarantee that action plans will fulfill their promise. But just as you can raise the probability that the written district curriculum is also the taught, tested, and learned curriculum, you also can increase the likelihood that your action plans for assessment will succeed. Here's how:

- Ensure your plan is grounded in the clear vision your team refined over the course of its study, using well-articulated beliefs about assessment as the foundation for that vision.
- Use the five actions self-analysis to focus on results by identifying long-term goals and specific, achievable milestones to chart the progress of your plan.
- Develop clear strategies aimed at reaching the goals and milestones with the required funding and other resources identified and allocated, if applicable.
- Identify the staff development required for teachers and administrators and plan for it to be readily available. Just as important, consider and plan for the time and conditions needed for adult learning to succeed. The aggregated results from the leaders' self-analysis of the Assessment Leadership Success Indicators (Activity 3.10) are one of the means to assist in the identification of the appropriate staff development.
- Recognize and communicate to others that the plan's sole purpose is to improve student learning, making it even more difficult to leave on a shelf.

If your school or district has a preferred planning process used successfully in the past, has a series of planning templates for documenting the goals and objectives, or follows a policy that guides the makeup of a planning team, we encourage your leadership team to put those tools to use here.

Prioritizing the Actions to Take

As you begin planning you may ask, "Where do we start? What should we do first, second, third . . . ?" The following questions may help give you consider the options:

What will be quickest or easiest to do immediately? The focus here is finding a scope of work that can be accomplished quickly yet contribute to realizing the vision.

For example, if your district has identified student achievement standards, but they are written in language that may be difficult for students or their families to understand, you can rewrite them into student- or family-friendly language, post them online or print them in the parent handbook, and regularly share them with students. This will immediately help both students and their parents. Students know where they are headed in their learning, and their parents will be better able to follow their children's progress and provide better ongoing feedback.

What will have the most impact? Examine your action plan and discuss the potential effect of your proposed actions. For example, you may decide that because quality professional development around assessment literacy is the underpinning of all five actions, refining your professional development program will have the greatest impact.

What actions are prerequisites to others? Ensuring all staff understands the difference between formative and summative assessment may be the starting place for your system because identifying the purpose for assessing is prerequisite to ensuring assessment quality.

What actions will support other district goals to improve learning? Assessment literacy can bring coherence and support to your district's or school's established goals and initiatives. Taking the time to establish the links between assessment literacy and response to intervention, or differentiated instruction, as two examples, can pay off in deeper understanding of how initiatives can connect and support each other.

TIME

The development of an action plan will vary depending on a number of factors. If all the stakeholders are present then the design of the plan may take 2 to 4 hours. If a core of leaders is present then the initial design may go over a period of days until all the necessary individuals have had a say in the design of the plan and agree to its components.

SUGGESTED ROOM SETUP

Tables and chairs for flow of discussion and a means to record and view the components of the plan as it unfolds

DIRECTIONS

Action Planning Templates

To provide a simple model for your action plan we have included sample planning templates for each of the five actions in Figure 3.7.

Top Section of the Action Plan Template

The top section of each of the five templates that follow crosses the various roles and levels in the organization of a school system. It is designed to help your team think about all the different levels and positions in the organization that could be called on to contribute to the plan's success. The intent is to foster thinking that reaches from the classroom to the boardroom in the design of your action plan. As an example, think about Action 1 and the work you need to do to balance your district assessment system. Within each cell of the table, enter what responsibilities fall to each player at each level. What is the school board's job relative to assessment balance, if any? The superintendent's? The teachers'?

Bottom Section of the Action Plan Template

The bottom section of each template is the action planning tool where you specify exactly what is to be done to create assessment balance and quality. Your team may have one goal for each of the five actions or several goals for each, depending entirely on your District Assessment System Self-Evaluation results. List here those activities supporting each goal for each of the five actions, describing the intended outcome, specific tasks required, the person(s) responsible, required resources, and the timeline for accomplishment.

A Point to Consider

Implementing a comprehensive action plan will unfold over time and will impact on multiple facets of the school organization. As with any dynamic system or organization when an impact is made in one area there will be reverberating impacts in other areas. Thus, it is essential that you revisit your action plan at least yearly to assess the effects of the changes and to make adjustments as needed to the plan to meet your intended outcomes.

Figure 3.7   Action Plan Templates

Action 1: Balance Your Assessment System

Roles and Responsibilities			
Position	**District Level**	**School Level**	**Classroom Level**
School Board			
Superintendent			
Curriculum Director			
Principals			
Curriculum and Instruction and Professional Development Staff			
Teachers			

Action Plan Goal				
Intended Outcome	**Specific Tasks Required**	**Person(s) Responsible**	**Required Resources**	**Time for Accomplishment**

Action 2: Continue to Refine Achievement Standards

Roles and Responsibilities			
Position	**District Level**	**School Level**	**Classroom Level**
School Board			
Superintendent			
Curriculum Director			
Principals			
Curriculum and Instruction and Professional Development Staff			
Teachers			

Action Plan Goal				
Intended Outcome	**Specific Tasks Required**	**Person(s) Responsible**	**Required Resources**	**Time for Accomplishment**

Action 3: Ensure Assessment Quality

Roles and Responsibilities			
Position	**District Level**	**School Level**	**Classroom Level**
School Board			
Superintendent			
Curriculum Director			
Principals			
Curriculum and Instruction and Professional Development Staff			
Teachers			

Action Plan Goal				
Intended Outcome	**Specific Tasks Required**	**Person(s) Responsible**	**Required Resources**	**Time for Accomplishment**

Roles and Responsibilities			
Position	**District Level**	**School Level**	**Classroom Level**
School Board			
Superintendent			
Curriculum Director			
Principals			
Curriculum and Instruction and Professional Development Staff			
Teachers			

Action Plan Goal				
Intended Outcome	**Specific Tasks Required**	**Person(s) Responsible**	**Required Resources**	**Time for Accomplishment**

Action 5: Link Assessment to Student Motivation With Assessment *for* Learning Strategies

Roles and Responsibilities			
Position	**District Level**	**School Level**	**Classroom Level**
School Board			
Superintendent			
Curriculum Director			
Principals			
Curriculum and Instruction and Professional Development Staff			
Teachers			

Action Plan Goal				
Intended Outcome	**Specific Tasks Required**	**Person(s) Responsible**	**Required Resources**	**Time for Accomplishment**

Available for download at **http://www.resources.corwin.com/ChappuisBalancedAssessment**

References

Ames, C. (1992). Classrooms: Goals, structures, and student motivation. *Journal of Educational Psychology, 84,* 261–271.

Andrade, H. (2010). Students as the definitive source of formative assessment: Academic self-assessment and the self-regulation of learning. In H. Andrade & G. Cizek (Eds.), *Handbook of formative assessment* (pp. 90–105). New York, NY: Routledge.

Arter, J. A., & Chappuis, J. (2006). *Creating and recognizing quality rubrics.* Portland, OR: Pearson.

Black, P., Harrison, C., Lee, C., Marshall, B., & Wiliam, D. (2002). *Working inside the black box: Assessment for learning in the classroom.* London, England: King's College.

Black, P., & Wiliam, D. (1998). Inside the black box: Raising standards through classroom assessment. *Phi Delta Kappan, 80*(2), 139–148.

Butler, R. (1988). Enhancing and undermining intrinsic motivation: The effects of task-involving evaluation on interest and performance. *British Journal of Educational Psychology, 58,* 1–14.

Cameron, J., & Pierce, D. P. (1994). Reinforcement, reward, and intrinsic motivation: A meta-analysis. *Review of Educational Research, 64*(3), 363–423.

Chappuis, J. (2009). *Seven strategies of assessment for learning.* Portland, OR: Pearson.

Chappuis, J. (2015). *Seven strategies of assessment for learning* (2nd ed.). Portland, OR: Pearson.

Chappuis, J., Stiggins, R. J., Chappuis, S., & Arter, J. (2012). *Classroom assessment for student learning: Doing it right—Using it well.* Portland, OR: Pearson.

Chappuis, J., & Chappuis, S. (2002). *Understanding school assessment: A parent and community guide to helping students learn.* Portland, OR: Pearson.

Chappuis, S., & Chappuis, J. (2008). The best value in formative assessment. *Educational Leadership, 65*(4), 14–18.

Council of Chief State School Officers. (2008). *Educational leadership policy standards: ISLLC 2008. As adopted by the National Policy Board for Educational Administration.* Washington, DC: Author.

Davidovich, R., Nikolay, P., Laugerman, B., & Commodore, C. (2010). *Beyond school improvement: Journey to innovative leadership.* Thousand Oaks, CA: Corwin.

DuFour, R., DuFour, R., Eaker, R., & Karhanek, G. (2004). *Whatever it takes: How professional learning communities respond when kids don't learn.* Bloomington, IN: National Educational Service.

Fullan, M. (2004, July). *Leadership and sustainability.* Presentation given at the Assessment Training Institute, Portland, OR.

Hattie, J., & Timperley, H. (2007). The power of feedback. *Review of Educational Research, 77*(1), 81–112. Retrieved from http://rer.sagepub.com/content/77/1/81

Kluger, A. N., & deNisi, A. (1996). The effects of feedback interventions on performance: A historical review, a meta-analysis, and a preliminary feedback intervention theory. *Psychological Bulletin, 119*(2), 254–284.

O'Connor, K. (2007). *A repair kit for grading: 15 fixes for broken grades*. Portland, OR: Pearson.

Office of Superintendent of Public Instruction. (1996). *Designing a district assessment system*. Olympia, WA: Author.

PDK International. (2015). *Testing doesn't measure up for Americans*. 47th Annual PDK/Gallup Poll. Bloomington, IN.

Ruiz-Primo, M. A., Furtak, E., Yin, Y., Ayala, C., & Shavelson, R. J. (2010). Formative assessment, motivation and science learning. In H. L. Andrade & G. J. Cizek (Eds.), *Handbook of formative assessment* (pp. 139–158). New York, NY: Routledge.

Sadler, D. R. (1989). Formative assessment and the design of instructional systems. *Instructional Science, 18,* 119–144.

Schneider, M. C., Egan, K. L., & Julian, M. W. (2013). Classroom assessment in the context of high-stakes testing. In J. McMillan (Ed.), *The SAGE handbook of research on classroom assessment* (pp. 55–70). Los Angeles, CA: SAGE.

Seligman, M. E. P. (1998). *Learned optimism: How to change your mind and your life*. New York, NY: Pocket Books.

Stiggins, R. J. (2014). *Revolutionize assessment: Engage students, inspire learning*. Thousand Oaks, CA: Corwin.

Stiggins, R. J., & Chappuis, J. (2011). *An introduction to student-involved assessment FOR learning* (6th ed.). Portland, OR: Pearson.

Index

Notes

Notes

CORWIN
A SAGE Publishing Company

Helping educators make the greatest impact

CORWIN HAS ONE MISSION: to enhance education through intentional professional learning.

We build long-term relationships with our authors, educators, clients, and associations who partner with us to develop and continuously improve the best evidence-based practices that establish and support lifelong learning.

Solutions you want. Experts you trust. Results you need.

 **AUTHOR CONSULTING**

Author Consulting

On-site professional learning with sustainable results! Let us help you design a professional learning plan to meet the unique needs of your school or district. www.corwin.com/pd

 **INSTITUTES**

Institutes

Corwin Institutes provide collaborative learning experiences that equip your team with tools and action plans ready for immediate implementation. www.corwin.com/institutes

 **ECOURSES**

eCourses

Practical, flexible online professional learning designed to let you go at your own pace. www.corwin.com/ecourses

 **READ2EARN**

Read2Earn

Did you know you can earn graduate credit for reading this book? Find out how: www.corwin.com/read2earn

Contact an account manager at (800) 831-6640 or visit **www.corwin.com** for more information.

 CORWIN